IMAGES OF ENGLAND

CHELTENHAM
VOLUME II

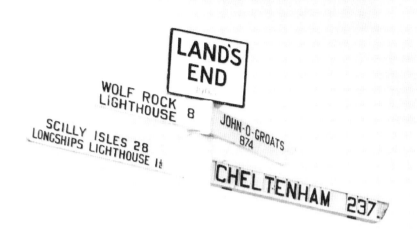

IMAGES OF ENGLAND

CHELTENHAM
VOLUME II

ELAINE HEASMAN

TEMPUS

This book is dedicated to my much-loved grandson Thomas, born 13 May 1996

Frontispiece: The author's sister and brother-in-law, Geraldine and Jack Smithers, at Land's End in the 1960s.

First published 2003

Tempus Publishing Limited
The Mill, Brimscombe Port,
Stroud, Gloucestershire, GL5 2QG
www.tempus-publishing.com

© Elaine Heasman, 2003

The right of Elaine Heasman to be identified as the Author
of this work has been asserted in accordance with the
Copyrights, Designs and Patents Act 1988.

British Library Cataloguing in Publication Data.
A catalogue record for this book is available from the British Library.

ISBN 0 7524 3085 8

Typesetting and origination by Tempus Publishing Limited.
Printed in Great Britain by Midway Colour Print, Wiltshire.

Contents

Acknowledgements

My sincere thanks to everyone who has helped with the production of this book, by lending photographs and postcards or offering advice and information. Special thanks to Geoff for his patience and assistance with the scanning of hundreds of photographs.

   If I have omitted anyone from the following list, please forgive me:

Eileen and Peter Allen, Bernard Avery, John Bartholomew, Carina Bibby, Jean Bint, Steven Blake, Cynthia Bracey, Sue Brasher, Joan Brown, the late Geoff Capper, the late Keith Caswell, Rene Cleaver, Vic Cole, Joyce and Les Cummings, the late Paul Dodwell, Derek Edwards, Beryl and John Elliott, Terry Enoch, Alan Gill, Jean Goddard, Peter Gunnell, James Hodsdon, John Hughes, Carol Jacob, Martin James, Doreen and the late Chubb Jewell, Jill Julier, Mick Kippin, Chris Lance, Marian Lewis, Roger Locke, Joyce Machin, Patricia Mackman, Lyn Mitchell, Mary Nelson, Doreen and Ray Niblett, Neil Parrack, Pat Pearce, Sue Rowbotham, Gill Selby, Joy Sharpe, John Smith, Keith Smith, Hugh Soar, Diana Stanley, Peter Stephens, Moya Thompson, Revd Brian Torode, Jill Waller, Brian White, Helen Willows, Jane Wood, David Young.

Introduction

I recently came across the photograph pictured as the frontispiece of my sister Geraldine and her husband John (known to everyone as 'Jack') Smithers, taken at Land's End in the early 1960s. Geoff and I visited Land's End in June of this year with grandson Thomas and stood by the very same signpost. The signpost is now in its own little enclosure instead of on the rocks but it did make me think: some things never change, some things have to change for good reasons and sometimes compromises have to be made. Visitors to Land's End can still have their photographs taken by the signpost but, in order to protect the environment and the eroding cliffs, not in the exact same spot as my sister did over forty years ago. Cheltenham is constantly changing and looking back through postcards and photographs one cannot help but wish some buildings had not been demolished and wonder how the destruction was justified. Undoubtedly, necessary improvements have been made, and thankfully, much of the town's history has been retained. It is there for those who care to look for it and volumes such as this hopefully encourage residents and visitors to explore a little more and seek out the past.

Since producing Volume I, I have been amazed by the response received from readers and should like to thank everyone who has taken the trouble and time to get in touch. I have enjoyed hearing your reminiscences and seeing your photographs, many of which are in this volume. I look forward to receiving your comments and any information you may have relating to the photographs now included. It is important that events are recorded accurately and names are added to group photographs where possible. The interest in local and family history continues to grow and photographs are a main source for any research. Please keep them coming!

One gentleman who made contact gave me more than a little surprise – rather a shock! In Volume I, I quoted from poems written by 'the late' Peter Gunnell. I am pleased to report that Peter contacted me to say that he was still alive and living in Bristol. Peter has since given me other poems written about Cheltenham, one is reproduced overleaf. Thoughts of home and childhood – we all have them. I remember wet leaves in the Promenade and long hot summer days at the Lido. I hope that this volume will recall a few memories for you too.

Elaine Heasman (née Worsfold)
July 2003

Contact address: Elaine Heasman, 7 Parr Close, Churchdown, Glos, GL3 1NH

Old Cheltenham

Winter came with chapped hands.
Welcomed it as I did the sight
Of the rear of the Municipal Buildings
Seen from Royal Well Road, dim,
Under gloomy Cheltenham skies.

Then there were the alleyways
Which led to the Parish Church
Away from the garish High Street.
Damp were the leaves underfoot,
Melancholy the Brewery steam.

And there were ghosts abroad:
Thoughts arrived; old fashioned
Sepia prints in a family album.
Feelings in the yellow gloom
Recognisably familiar to me.

That led back to childhood:
Weary, completing some errand,
My making a beeline for home –
Drawn, not only by hunger, but
Warmth and love, like a Magnet!

by Peter Gunnell
November 1988

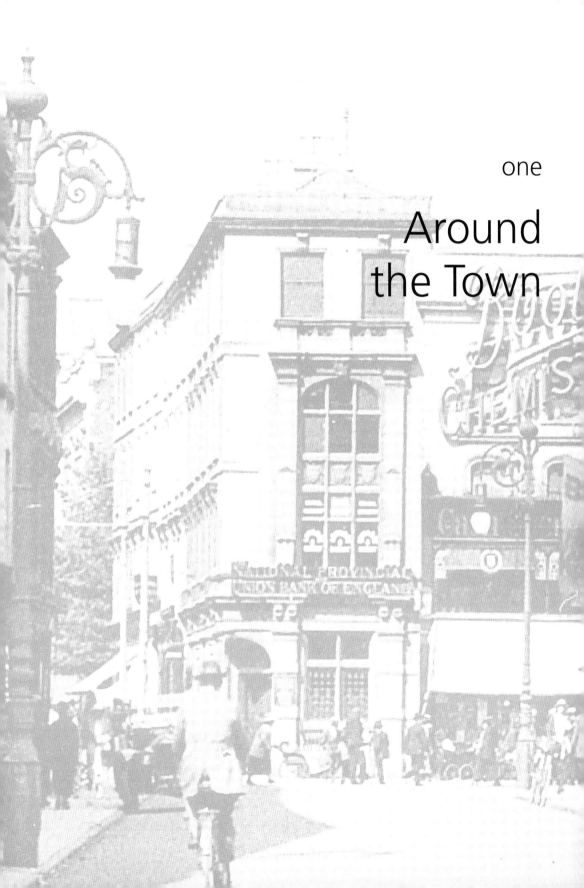

one

Around the Town

Section I – Places

Above: There is little doubt that the discovery of the spa waters led to the development of the small town of Cheltenham as a popular resort attracting the well-to-do and influential of the eighteenth and early nineteenth centuries. This card produced by Norman Bros. Ltd of Bennington Street shows Cheltenham, in the first decade of the twentieth century, described as 'Queen of the Spas' in order to attract visitors to the town. This picture is of the newly built Town Hall, where the waters could be taken whilst seated in comparatively luxurious surroundings and where fine music and pleasant conversation would be enjoyed. The card lists other attractions of pre-war Cheltenham: beautiful gardens, daily concerts, opera houses, golf, hunting, tennis, croquet and as a special feature – motor tours.

Opposite top left: St Mary's Parish Church contains possibly the longest memorial to one family. Cheltenham owes much to the Skillicorne family, not least to Captain Henry Skillicorne who came to Cheltenham in 1738 with his second wife Elizabeth Mason, and saw the potential of the 'Old Spring'. As stated on the memorial, he 'brought this most salutary Water to just estimation & extensive Use, and ever presiding with esteem in the Walks, saw it visited with Benefit, by the greatest Persons of the Age, and so established its Reputation.' Henry died in 1763 and his son William in 1803.

Henry's great grandson, William Nash Skillicorne (1807-87), became Cheltenham's first Mayor in 1876.

Opposite top right: Old Well Walk as laid out by Captain Skillicorne with its trees, promenades and the little pump house from where the waters could be taken. At the end of the walk is St Mary's Church, the only medieval building in Cheltenham. It is thought that a Saxon church may have previously existed on the site.

In Memory of Captain HENRY SKILLICORNE deceased born at Kirk Lonnon in the Isle of Man in 1678 taught by D.r WILSON Bishop, and justly called the good Bishop of that Island.When young he went to Sea,and was many Years in the employ of and concern'd with JACOB ELTON Esq.r Merchant in Bristol, whose Relation SARAH GOLDSMITH of that City he married. She dying in Childbed with two Children.He in 1731 married ELIZABETH MASON, then of Bristol, Daughter of WILL.m MASON of Cheltenham Gentleman by MARGARET SURMAN Daughter of JOHN SURMAN of Tredington in this County Esq.r He quiting the Sea after 40 Years Service, they resided together some Years at Bristol, and in 1738 came to live upon their Estate in this Town. where he gave his Mind to increase the Knowledge & extend the Use of Cheltenham Spa, which became his Property. He found the Old Spring, open and exposed to the Weather.He made the Well there as it now is, made the Walks, and planted the Trees, of the Upper & lower Parades, and by Conduct ingenuous, & Manners attentive. He with the Aid of Many worthy Persons of the Town & Neighbourhood, brought this most salutary Water, to just estimation, & extensive Use. and ever presiding with esteem in the Walks, saw it visited with Benefit. by the greatest Persons of the Age, and so established its Reputation, that his Present Most Gracious Majesty King GEORGE The Third, with His most amiable Queen CHARLOTTE & the Princesses ROYAL AUGUSTA & ELIZABETH their Daughters, visited it drinking the Water, & residing From the 12.th day of July, to the 16.th day of August both inclusive 1788 in the Lodge House built by WILL.m SKILLICORNE the Proprietor thereof, and of the Spa, Son of Captain SKILLICORNE. on his Bays hill, near thereto for & then & now in Lease, to the Right Honourable Earl FAUCONBERG, Who receiving Benefit from this Water, for many Years spread its good Name.W.m MILLER Esq.r The Tenant of the Spa, & others of the Town, erected new Buildings, paved, cleansed, & lighted the Street, encouraged by the Gentlemen of the Neighbourhood, making new Roads.The King discovered the new Spring like the Old, which his Majesty steaned & secured, and built 17 Rooms at the Lodge House, at his own Expence, and graciously gave to M.r SKILLICORNE. in whose Ground near the House it was, at the instance of Earl FAUCONBERG Captain SKILLICORNE was buried the 18.th of October 1763 with his Son HENRY, by his last Wife, at the West Door on the Inside of this Church. Aged 84 Years. He was an excellent Sea Man, of tryed Courage. He visited most of the great Trading Ports of the Mediterranean up the Archipelago, Morea & Turkey, Spain, Portugal, & Venice, and several of the North American Ports, Philadelphia, and Boston, and Holland. and could do Business in seven Tongues.He was of great Regularity & Probity, & so temperate, as never to have been once intoxicated. Religious without Hypocrisy, Grave without Austirity, of a Chearful Conversation without Levity. A kind Husband & tender Father. Tall, erect, robust, & Active. From an Ill treated Wound while a Prisoner. after an Engagement at Sea, He became a strict Valetudenarian He lived and dyed an honest Man.
M.rs ELIZABETH SKILLICORNE a Quaker, was buried in the Quakers Grave Yard, upon the 14.th of April 1779. A Virtuous Woman, A good Wife & tender Mother. WILLIAM SKILLICORNE Esq.r died April 12.th 1803. Aged 66 Years.

Interestingly, this trade token dated 1812 shows a similar view of Well Walk. Its value is one penny and a pound note is offered by John Bishop & Co. for 240 tokens.

North Place Chapel, *c.* 1900. Portland Chapel in North Place was built in 1816 by Robert Capper. In June 1819 Capper gave the chapel to the Countess of Huntingdon's trustees. In the 1850s the first British school to be established by the Nonconformists was set up here. The church has not been a place of worship for a number of years. From 1998 the building has been used by Chapel Rock Gym and in 2003, after extensive refurbishment, Chapel Spa has been created. With its treatment rooms, pool and steam room, the facilities of a traditional spa town are once again on offer.

Opposite above: A little-known memorial to the Skillicorne family exists today in this peaceful oasis behind the Town Hall. The Skillicorne Garden was captured here on camera in 1997 with its special 'visitors' – sheep by the controversial sculptor Sophie Ryder. Her work is not always popular but, over the years, Sophie has provided much enjoyment and amusement to many people.

Right: Captain Skillicorne's Royal Well and adjoining Assembly Rooms built by his son William were demolished and replaced by a new Pump Room, *c.* 1850. This building, together with the Royal Well Gardens, were later purchased by the Ladies' College and the Princess Hall was constructed on this site between 1895 and 1897.

THE PRINCESS HALL LADIES COLLEGE
CHELTENHAM

On the morning of Tuesday 4 May 1971 Her Majesty Queen Elizabeth the Queen Mother flew into Staverton Airport to be received by His Grace the Duke of Beaufort (her Majesty's Lieutenant for the County of Gloucester), Her Grace the Duchess of Beaufort and Mr E.P.B. White, the Chief Constable of Gloucestershire. Her Majesty was driven to Cheltenham Ladies' College where she officially opened the new Sixth Form wing. She then proceeded to Pittville to formally declare the new Pittville Swimming Pools open. In this photograph, Miss M.G. Hampshire, the Ladies' College Principal, is being presented to Her Majesty. Standing behind is His Worship the Mayor of Cheltenham Councillor Lt Col. E.J.M. Eldridge. On the steps, the mace is carried ahead of the proceedings.

Above and below: Cotswold House in Fauconberg Road, built in 1937, is the official residence of the Principal of the College. At the outbreak of war in 1939 the majority of the Ladies' College buildings were requisitioned. Only the Principal's House, the College Secretary's Office and the Swimming Baths were retained. Miss Margaret Popham, as Principal, worked tirelessly to keep the school operating in Cheltenham throughout the war and in 1940 she gave up her house to be used by the Domestic Science girls. Miss Popham retired in 1953, the centenary year of the founding of the College. She is remembered for introducing the new green uniform.

This photograph taken of the girls and staff of Glenlee in 1965 has been signed by all those present – too many to print here. Glenlee was the first purpose-built Ladies' College boarding house, completed in 1901 at a cost of £13,600. The architects were Waller. In 1939 Glenlee was requisitioned by the Government and remained so until 1944. For part of this time Glenlee was used as an American army hospital. Mrs Garner was Housemistress of Glenlee from 1945 to 1967.

An early photograph taken by E.M. Bailey, a Cheltenham photographer operating from premises in the High Street prior to 1914. The Ladies' College owned playing fields near Christ Church. The gasholders in Gloucester Road are clearly visible in the background.

Right: Another E.M. Bailey photograph, on a card posted in November 1907, just a few months after this memorial to the men who had served in the Boer War in South Africa was unveiled. The memorial was sculpted by R.L. Boulton & Sons Ltd. The railings around the garden were designed and made by R.E. & C. Marshall Ltd, a Cheltenham firm established in 1822, which operated in the High Street and later in Royal Well Lane and closed in 1954. Behind the memorial is Scarborough House and on the corner of Post Office Lane, Promenade House, which still survives today as Yates' Wine Bar.

Opposite above: Cheltenham's Promenade and Drive dated 4 September 1874. This elegant tree-lined avenue was established in the early nineteenth century as a carriageway connecting the High Street to the new Sherborne Spa (where the Queen's Hotel now stands). Hotels, terraces and large villas were built along the avenue. Gradually, the Promenade developed into the commercial area it is today. The trees remain an important part of the Promenade. As the older trees have to be felled they are replaced by new ones.

Opposite below: This pre-First World War view of the Promenade area we know as the Municipal Offices and the Long Gardens is markedly different in that there were, as yet, no memorials or statues in the gardens (which still have their railings). The buildings were, at this time, all residential properties and the gardens were for use by the owners of the terrace. Built in the 1820s, these houses were originally known as Harward's Buildings after the developer Samuel Harward.

Above: Invoice for five guineas, 6 July 1861, W.T. Smith's, Shawl, Cloak & Millinery Rooms, 3 Promenade Villas. Note the proviso 'For Ready Money Only'. Mr Smith has signed across the one penny Victoria stamp by way of receipt on 22 July 1862.

Left: Correspondence from agents for the Union Fire & Life Insurance Offices, March 1894. The Cheltenham Auction Mart and Pantechnicon is advertised in 1863 in *Norman's History of Cheltenham* by John Goding as having 'upwards of 30 large & dry apartments … for the storage of large or small quantities of household furniture, pictures, linen, wines, books, luggage, carriages etc by the year, month or week'.

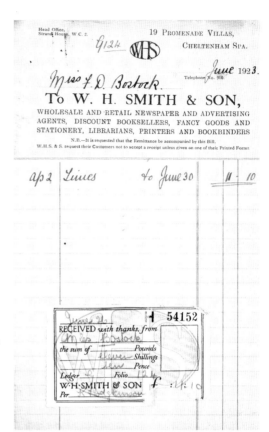

Head Office,
Strand House, W.C. 2.

G124 WHS

19 PROMENADE VILLAS,
CHELTENHAM SPA.

June 1923.

Telephone No. 910.

Miss F. D. Bostock.

To W. H. SMITH & SON,

WHOLESALE AND RETAIL NEWSPAPER AND ADVERTISING
AGENTS, DISCOUNT BOOKSELLERS, FANCY GOODS AND
STATIONERY, LIBRARIANS, PRINTERS AND BOOKBINDERS

N.B.—It is requested that the Remittance be accompanied by this Bill.
W.H.S. & S. request their Customers not to accept a receipt unless given on one of their Printed Forms

ap 2 | Times | to June 30 | 11 - 10

54152

RECEIVED with thanks, from
Miss Bostock
the sum of _____ Pounds
_____ Shillings
_____ Pence
Ledger ____ Folio ____
W·H·SMITH & SON
Per _____

Right and below: Many readers will remember when W.H. Smith & Son was located in the Promenade. This invoice dating from June 1923, apparently for three months' delivery of *The Times* newspaper, proudly includes Cheltenham Spa in the address. The row of shops pictured below includes many old favourites from the 1960s: Banks, W.H. Smith & Son, F.J. Foice & Co., Alfred Hurran and Maryon.

Christmas shopping and lights in a 1990s view of the Promenade. The original façade of Cavendish House, dating back to the early 1900s, was replaced by the present modern frontage, constructed between 1964 and 1966.

The Minotaur and The Hare, the almost 10ft-high, 2.5-ton bronze work of Cirencester sculptor Sophie Ryder and cast in Chalford at the Pangolin foundry, became a permanent fixture in this position in the Promenade in 1997. £50,000 was raised to keep the statue in the town. Objections are often raised to its presence and many call it an obscenity but many have grown to love it. In the background is Hoopers department store, which took over the former main post office site in 1987, but closed in July 2003, the lease having been acquired by Ottakar's booksellers. The impressive building dates from 1832 and was originally a private residence, then later it became the Imperial Hotel and in 1856 the Imperial Club. The General Post Office was housed here for more than one hundred years.

James Anderton is listed in 1902 as a toy dealer at 145 High Street. It is interesting that in the early 1900s this postcard was published by Jas Anderton showing what was then a one-hundred-year-old view of the High Street. Another hundred years on and we too are fascinated by views over a century old.

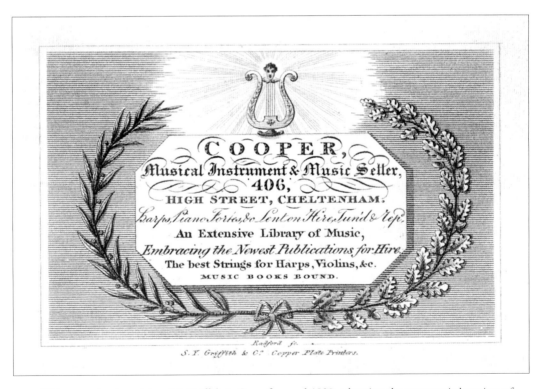

This engraving by printers S.J. Griffith & Co., of around 1830, advertises the many varied services of Cooper, Musical Instrument & Music Seller of 406 High Street.

Left: This image is taken from a postcard view included in full in the author's first volume of *Cheltenham* (page 21). Considerable interest was shown in the buildings on the corner of North Street as seen from the Colonnade before development of this area. In this close-up, Boots Chemist can be seen clearly in the High Street. The corner building is occupied by the National Provincial Union Bank of England and the outline of the buildings can be traced round into North Street.

Below: This postcard view clearly shows Boots' corner in the 1900s before any redevelopment. A tram is travelling along the High Street and the old Grammar School building can be seen in the distance. The town clock hangs aloft. The Empress Tea Stores occupy Littlewoods' corner or where readers may remember Wards Department Store stood for many years. On the corner of the Colonnade a sign indicates towards the Promenade. The shops at this time maintained the line of the High Street.

This view, taken around 1918, is looking towards the High Street, again before any redevelopment has taken place. The bank on the corner of North Street and Boots just inside the High Street are clearly visible, also the impressive frontage of Dodwell & Sons on the right of the card on the corner with Clarence Street.

A lovely close-up of Dodwell & Sons, newsagents and stationers, at 361 High Street, prior to the redevelopment of the Colonnade corner in the 1930s and demolition of these premises. The staff stand in the shop doorway for this photograph to be taken. Dodwell's calls itself 'The News Depot' and headlines such as 'Premier Meets Miners' can be seen on the boards outside for papers including *The Mirror*, *The Daily Graphic* and *The Times*. Saxone Shoe Co. Ltd adjoins Dodwell's in Clarence Street.

Where are the tourists? There are no takers for the deckchairs today. This photograph of Neptune's Fountain in the Promenade was taken on 22 August 1937. The former Imperial Spa behind displays a SOLD notice. This building had more recently been used as piano showrooms by Dale, Forty & Co. Ltd. Also visible are the frontages of Madame Hilda Bell, furrier, and Miss Gertrude Doxsey, selling machine-knitted goods.

No deckchairs now on 19 September 1937. Demolition has begun on the Imperial Spa site. The skyline is changing and chinks of daylight are apparent through Miss Doxsey's knitwear shop.

26 September 1937. Nothing but a big open space behind Neptune! The building now revealed is the former Royal Well Methodist Chapel.

An aerial view of the site behind Neptune's Fountain, looking towards St George's Road. The Regal Cinema was built here, later to become the ABC. The small building on the corner of St George's Road occupied by Pate's & Co. survived until the 1990s. The building behind is the Royal Well Methodist Chapel demolished in 1965. The architects for the cinema were William R. Glen and Leslie C. Norton and the builders were William T. Nicholls of Gloucester. The cinema opened in January 1939 and closed in 1981. The River Chelt runs beneath this site.

Note: the four photographs on these pages were taken by the late Keith Caswell who spent most of his working life as a photographer in Cheltenham and sadly died in July 2003.

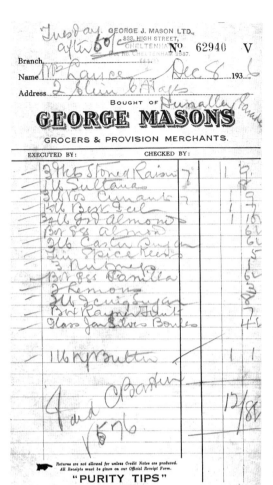

Left: George Masons in the High Street will be remembered by many into the 1960s. This invoice from December 1936 would appear to be for a Christmas cake. The address is 333 High Street, which became 254 after subsequent renumbering of the High Street in the 1950s.

Below: This early view by Burrow, *c.* 1900, is clearly advertising Cossens & Knight, 353 High Street. In 1902, Cossens & Knight are listed at this address as booksellers & fancy dealers. The old grammar school building is a prominent feature of the Lower High Street at this time.

This is a view of the High Street taken between the wars. Dunn & Co. Hat Makers occupied a quaint Swiss-style building on the corner of Winchcombe Street from 1926, but this building was to be demolished along with others on the east side of Winchcombe Street in the 1960s.

In this view of the Lower High Street from the late 1950s Albert Lusty's van is parked outside the family hardware business. Many local residents will have purchased paraffin and other such products from Mr Lusty on his rounds around Cheltenham. Boots Chemist had a branch in the Lower High Street at this time and other favourites are here: J.R. Tapp – the noted pie shop, Miss Binder stationer & sub-post office, Bloodworth's, Emes refreshments, Adcock & Son, Colyer's ladies' hairdressers and Grey's newsagent. Two of the many public houses of the Lower High Street – the King's Head and the Royal Oak – can also be seen.

POST OFFICE
SAVINGS
BANK

LOWER HIGH ST.
CHELTENHAM
6558

Quote the above particulars on all
letters to the Savings Department
and on all withdrawal forms

STATE SECURITY

Left: A Post Office Savings Bank book
from the Lower High Street Branch.

Opposite above: A contrasting view of the Lower High Street captured in the year 2000 by Sue Brasher
as part of a series of photographs taken in the Millennium year. Although small businesses still feature in
this area, McDonald's and other fast-food outlets are now popular and there are numerous charity shops
to be found. Tesco's supermarket is on the right of the photograph.

Opposite below: The shops in this part of the High Street, looking down to the Strand with the Bath
Road junction on the left, look very different in this view captured by the photographer E.M. Bailey,
c. 1900. At this time the numbers ran consecutively down the High Street. A.R. Caudle at 74 offered
hats, hosiery and tailoring. Next door, at 73 were Newbold & Newton, Stationers & Post Office.
Mrs S. Newton is listed as the sub-postmistress in 1902. In that year, there would have been no fewer
than six postal deliveries daily in the town, starting at 7 a.m. and continuing until 7.50 p.m. (weekends
may have been a little different) and the cost of postage inland for a postcard was one halfpenny. Across
the road on the corner of Bath Road part of the premises of Henry George Norton & Co. can just be
seen. They were listed in 1902 as Ironmongers at 416 High Street and Cycle Agents at 2-5 Bath Road.

This lovely drawing by G.A. Underwood, architect, of the Plough Hotel as a coaching inn, was published by S.Y. Griffith & Co. in 1826 in their *New Historical Description of Cheltenham*. In the 1820s, 'Royal Mails and Light and Elegant Post Coaches' travelled daily to Gloucester, London and Milford and every day except Sunday to Shrewsbury & Holyhead, Birmingham, Manchester, Liverpool, Bath and Bristol. A thrice-weekly service was offered to Warwick & Leamington and Southampton. A two-day coach went to London daily, sleeping at Oxford. The Berkeley Hunt, New Coach to London, was advertised leaving as every morning at 6 a.m., arriving in London, Ludgate Hill, at 4.30 p.m. for dinner.

No longer a coaching inn but still very popular, the Plough Hotel and Plough Garage, Cheltenham Spa, now welcomes the motor car. Note the 4-digit telephone number. This card was produced by Ed. J. Burrow & Co. Ltd.

Right: In 1950, when this card was posted to Plymouth, the cost of postage had risen to 2d. In this rather unusual view the High Street appears to buzz with activity and shoppers are obviously enjoying the summer sunshine. A policeman directs traffic coming out of Pittville Street and along the High Street. Cars are also directed to the left down Regent Street to the Opera House and the car park. At the bottom right the sign of Fredk Wright Ltd, tobacconists, can just be seen. At this time, two hotels, namely The Crown and The Lamb, together with the Palace Theatre, could also be found in this stretch of the High Street.

Below: Having cost £23 million the Regent Arcade opened in November 1984 on the site of the Plough Hotel and Yard, and the Regent Garage. It had been hoped to retain the façade of the former Plough Hotel in the development but sadly it was not possible. A mosaic from the hotel was, however, saved and restored and a gold sculpture of the Gloster jet aeroplane, part of the prototype of which had been constructed on the old Regent Motors site, is displayed in the main arcade. This photograph was also taken by Sue Brasher in 2000.

Above: The New Club was built as an exclusive gentlemen's club in 1874 and stood at the corner of the Promenade and Imperial Square. In the 1900s the Club was described as having 'somewhat exclusive and limited membership', and as being 'an important focus of men's society', 'particularly for those gentlemen of leisure who, with their families, form the first circle of Cheltenham's social life'. In 1970, the New Club relocated to Atherstone Lawn, Montpellier Parade. In this photograph the contents are being moved by the local furniture removal company Barnby Bendall & Co. Ltd. This firm closed in 1976.

Left : Mr Holmes, the doorman of the New Club for many years, on the final day. Note the fine detail of the ironwork of the canopied porch.

A glimpse of the elegant interior of the New Club. Some of the furniture and fittings were removed to the new premises but much was destroyed or lost when the building was demolished.

September 1970. The last bricks of a very fine building, which many local people feel should never have been demolished. In its place, a modern office block, The Quadrangle, was built.

Verdun Private Hotel

Pleasantly situated in the best part of Promenade. Convenient for Ladies' College, Shops and Station. Gas fires in bedrooms. Electric light. Constant hot water.

Resident Proprietress :
MRS F. A. COSSENS

PROMENADE, CHELTENHAM SPA

This advertisement appeared in a Cheltenham Parish Church guidebook. The hotel at 113 Promenade later changed its name to Hotel Verdun (Mrs F.A. Cossens was still listed as the resident proprietress in 1940).

Tate's Private Hotel,
Cheltenham
(Between the New Club and the Ladies' College).
Visitors received on pension at **Daily** *or Weekly Terms.*
Table d'Hôte at Separate Tables.
Handsome and Commodious Drawing Rooms, Reading Room, and Comfortable Smoke Room for Gentlemen. *Inclusive Terms.*

Tate's Private Hotel occupied 1–4 Promenade Terrace in 1902 and situated 'between the New Club and the Ladies' College' was most convenient for visitors to the town. This advertisement appeared in *Cheltenham: The Garden Town* (third edition 1903-4), written by Dr J.H. Garrett, Medical Officer of Health for Cheltenham, and published by Edward J. Burrow, Pomfret House, Cheltenham.

Section II – People and Events

Above: In 2003, the James' family has good reason to celebrate. Since 1853 there has been a chemist bearing the family name serving the people of Cheltenham. This photograph represents part of a display mounted in 1953 at C. & P. James Ltd former premises in the Promenade. This year the family very proudly celebrates 150 years in business.

Right: The James' family continued to operate from 5 Promenade for many years (29 Promenade after renumbering). This photograph provides a glimpse of the interior of C. & P. James Ltd, the Promenade Pharmacy, as it was some years before it closed in 1970. James Pharmacy continues the family tradition today at 19 St George's Road.

Above and below: A scarcely recognisable view of the Lower Promenade at the turn of the century. Martin & Co. Jewellers in the Colonnade as we know them today can be seen in the distance. In 1900, this part of the Promenade was predominantly residential. However, businesses were operating behind the railings. The General Post Office moved into the premises of the former Imperial Club in 1874. At 5 Promenade, Joseph James was practising as a homeopathic chemist. Joseph was previously at 1 Promenade Place, where he had been apprenticed to Edwin Wheeler. Advertisements for Joseph's remedies appeared in the *Cheltenham and District Post Office Directories* for the 1890s (see below). Joseph also prepared James' Dog Powders and other potions for dogs and cats, which were available from all chemists or by post from Mr James. Joseph's son Clarence joined him in 1895 after studying at a London College of Pharmacy. Joseph died in 1904. Later, Mr Percy James, Joseph's nephew, joined Clarence and C. & P. James Ltd was formed.

COUNT MATTEI'S ELECTRO-
HOMŒOPATHIC REMEDIES.

JOSEPH JAMES, 1, Promenade Place,

Cheltenham, who has visited COUNT MATTEI at his Castle, near Bologna, has been appointed his Agent, and will forward to anyone desirous of testing these REMEDIES, Five of those most used, which will treat the majority of Diseases from which we suffer.

POST FREE, with Directions for Use. price 5/9.

Every bottle or tube bears the Trade Mark. "The Castle," WITHOUT WHICH NONE ARE GENUINE.

TRADE MARK.   VIII.

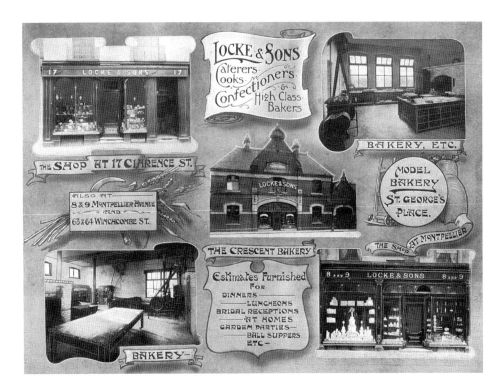

Above and below: The advertisement above is from 1912. Henry Locke was a baker in the 1840s. His two sons Henry John and Howard Harry later joined him in business. The original bakery and shop of Locke's Bakeries were at 17 Clarence Street. By 1894, the company had also taken over premises at 8/9 Montpellier Avenue. In 1905, the firm moved to a new purpose-built bakery in St George's Place known as The Crescent Bakery. In May 1895, Henry Locke & Sons won the Gold Medal for Wedding Cakes at the prestigious London Cookery Exhibition. In the summer of 1889, Locke's provided the catering for the wedding of the daughter of the then Mayor of Cheltenham Alderman Newman Burfoot Thoyts.

Above: In the early years deliveries were by horse and cart. In July 1895, the wedding cake pictured above travelled all the way to the village of Arthog, near Dolgelly, in North Wales, for the wedding reception.

Left: At least four of the bakers photographed here in front of the delivery truck in the yard of The Crescent Bakery are known to be Locke family members. Standing, from left to right: Howard Henry Locke, Gilbert Martin Locke (both grandsons of the founder Henry Locke), -?-. Seated: -?-, Howard Harry Locke (son of the founder), Cecil Alton Locke (grandson of the founder). From the 1950s to the early '80s, Locke's products were supplied to many of the major hotels, schools and stores in Cheltenham. The famous Locke Dripping Cake was a special favourite. The firm closed in 1984.

The Revd Beynon Phillips, Minister of Cambray Baptist Church 1895 to 1908. He started his ministry by renovating the Chapel during which time services were held in the High Street Assembly Rooms. These renovations included introducing coloured glass windows, decorating, electric light to replace the gasoliers, and the current iron railings at the front of the building. The Revd Phillips started a Literary Society at Cambray, which had a membership of up to 100. He also introduced and edited the monthly *Church Magazine*. In 1905, when the chapel celebrated its Jubilee, the Revd Phillips compiled a history of the building. At that time, membership stood at 600, with a Sunday School of 500.

The Revd Phillips resigned in June 1908 to move to Newport, leaving Cheltenham in July. Parting gifts to him from the congregation were money, a clock, a desk chair, a desk, pen and inkstand, blotter and framed photographs. This card shows the Desk Set presented to the Revd Phillips by his Sunday afternoon Bible Class, 24 July 1908.

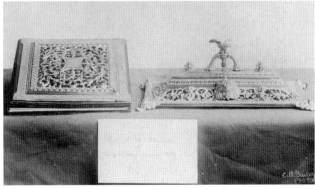

Clock Set presented to the Revd Phillips. The photographer was again E.M. Bailey and the card was posted on 30 July 1908 to Mrs W.P. Honeysett, c/o Mr W. Howlett, 3 Clarence Street. William Howlett is listed as a watchmaker.

Cambray Baptist Chapel in Cambray Place was designed by Henry Dangerfield, the Borough Surveyor, with an Italian-style façade and elevation. It was built in 1853-5 with 1,000 seatings at a cost of £3,400. In 1896, the Revd Beynon Phillips organised the purchase and demolition of Essex Cottages and Essex Villa, at the rear of the chapel, in Rodney Road. The New Hall was built in 1898 as a lecture theatre, where the Sunday School met and week-night meetings were held, as well as social events. The architect of the Hall was Mr H.W. Chatters of Knight & Chatters. The writer of this card, believed to have been posted in 1905, describes how he 'goes through the gate at the side of the chapel to school on a Sunday at 9.40 a.m.'

Arthur John Byard and Winifred (Win) Mary Sparrow were both baptised by the Revd Beynon Phillips at Cambray on the same day in 1905. On 7 March 1911, he married them. This photograph of the wedding party is believed to have been taken in the garden of 7 Oxford Place, London Road. Included in the group are: Joyce Handy, Win's grandmother; Edie James, her bridesmaid; George Byard, Arthur's brother, and his wife; Ernest Handy. When war broke out in 1914, Arthur enlisted in the Royal Army Medical Corps and died in France in 1917. Another brother, Francis, was also killed in the war in 1918.

The New Cheltenham Steam Fire Engine of the 'Greenwich Gem' type was presented to the town on behalf of Mrs Theobold in 1904. On 1 October, a crowd gathered in Montpellier Gardens for the presentation and demonstration of the Engine. Major Boyce Podmore and Captain Such were among the officers. The Mayor and visiting brigades watched the display and the Cheltenham Fire Brigade Band played.

Cheltenham Fire Brigade Steamer dry drill. This photograph of No. 2 Section of the brigade was taken in the Corporation yard in St James' Square, *c.* 1906-7. Second from the right is Fireman Driver Ernest C. S. Niblett who served with the brigade for thirty-three years, living in the fire station for many of them. The Fire Brigade moved from the St James' premises to Keynsham Road in 1959.

Gilsmiths Hippodrome (after Mr Cecil Gill Smith) opened in 1913 in Albion Street. It advertised twice-nightly performances, offering a variety of theatre and shows. This photograph, taken during the First World War, is by A.R. Nesbitt of 463 High Street. When the Hippodrome was built the original façade of the former Conservative Club building was retained. In 1919, the theatre was renovated and renamed the Coliseum. In the 1920s and '30s, as film became more popular, the Coliseum was possibly Cheltenham's main venue for live theatre. However, in 1931, the Coliseum succumbed and switched to films. During the Second World War, the Coliseum advertised programmes 'continuous daily from 2.15p.m.' with 'Paramount latest topical news in each programme'.

CHELTENHAM
HOSPITAL
EXTENSION
BALL

COMMITTEE :

Mr. J. G. D. Currie,   Mr. T. D. Deighton,
Dr. John Howell,   Mr. J. P. F. Lloyd,
Mrs. J. G. D. Currie,   Mrs. J. P. F. Lloyd.

TUESDAY, APRIL 6TH. 1937

TOWN HALL,
CHELTENHAM.

SHENTONS PRINTING WORKS, CHELTENHAM

MARIUS B. WINTER'S BAND

PATRONS :

Rev. R. H. M. Bouth,   Mrs. Heber-Percy,
Mr. John Howell,   Dr. J. P. Collins,
Mr. J. S. Robinson,   Mr. Ernest Fieldhouse,
Major Stephen Mitchell.

PROGRAMME.

1. Foxtrot
2. Slow Foxtrot
3. Waltz
4. Paul Jones
5. Foxtrot
6. Slow Foxtrot
7. Waltz

FIRST SUPPER, 11 o'clock.

8. Foxtrot
9. Foxtrot
10. Foxtrot
11. Slow Foxtrot
12. Foxtrot
13. Waltz

SECOND SUPPER, 12.15 o'clock.

14. Foxtrot
15. Foxtrot
16. Slow Foxtrot
17. Foxtrot
18. Foxtrot

1st Extra............ 2nd Extra

Corporation of Cheltenham.

MAY 21st. 1934.

WHIT-MONDAY

Carnival

PROGRAMME OF NON-STOP
MUSIC & ENTERTAINMENT

Souvenir Programme ~ 2d.

Above and opposite below: Cheltenham people have always been keen and willing to assist with fund-raising for good causes, not least for the town's hospitals. These illustrations are just a few examples of fund-raising events. The General Hospital in Sandford Road was opened in 1849. Previously, Idmiston House (later Normandy House) in the Lower High Street had been used as a hospital.

Parish School infant children performing *The Pied Piper of Hamlyn*, *c.* 1914. Lilian Jakeway is sitting in the second row, fourth from the left. This card was sent, written by Lilian's father Frank, to Frank, her brother, who was then serving with the 7th Gloucestershire Regiment, with the message, 'from Lilly wishing you many Happy Returns of the Day'. Frank was killed in action in Gallipoli on 12 August 1915, aged twenty.

Parish Church Infant School, *c.* 1929. This school in St James' Square took boys and girls up to the age of seven. The boys were then transferred to the Junior School in Devonshire Street. Fred Cummings, aged about five, is seated in the middle of the second row.

The above is taken from the chorus of the Grammar School song written by L.J. Cheney. Richard Pate founded a grammar school in the High Street in 1578. The original building was replaced in 1889 by another on the same site, which was itself demolished in the 1960s when the Grammar School moved out of town to Hesters Way.

A Cheltenham Grammar School Rugby team pose for their photograph. On the reverse of the card 'Jack Hannis Feb 1921' is written. Can any reader identify Jack?

Boys watch as a brave competitor attempts the Water Jump, *c.* 1945. The playing field used by the Grammar School at this time was at St Mark's.

Above: Bennington Hall, St Margaret's Road. This photograph, by E.H. Stallard, taken in 1923, is of the Bennington Hall Gym Club. Lilian Jakeway is kneeling in front on the right and her younger sister Ivy is standing second from left in the back row. Both girls attended the Central School in Gloucester Road. Note the gymslips being worn.

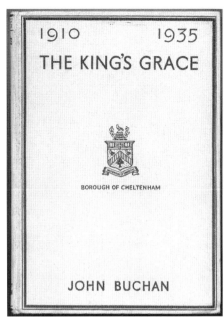

Above and below: The Mayor of Cheltenham, Councillor E.L. Ward JP, encouraged the people of Cheltenham to celebrate the 25th Anniversary of the Accession of HM King George V on 6 May 1935. A whole day of events was planned for the town starting with a Jubilee Service in St Matthew's Church at 10.30 a.m. followed by fun fairs, band concerts, racing on Prestbury Park, motor gymkhana, motorcycle football and open-air dancing. At 10 p.m. Jubilee Beacons on Leckhampton Hill and Cleeve Hill were lit. Finally, the Grand Jubilee Ball continued until 3 a.m. Senior schoolchildren were given copies of John Buchan's book imprinted with the Cheltenham crest, and younger children received specially packed chocolate, as illustrated below.

Opposite below: Cheltenham Art Students constructed a giant Venus, 25ft high, for their Art Students' Ball held at the Town Hall in December 1927. It had a modelled head and a canvas body and was built around a cubist framework. This photograph was taken outside the School of Art in St Margaret's Road. The photographer was a local man, Harold Stokes, from St Paul's Road.

STOCK CERTIFICATE.

CERTIFICATE Nº S 251

AMOUNT OF STOCK £ 25

REPRESENTED BY 250 UNITS OF 2/- EACH.

THE CHERSONESE (F.M.S.) ESTATES, Limited.

INCORPORATED UNDER THE Companies (Consolidation) Acts 1908-1917.

CAPITAL £350,000.

Divided into £350,000 STOCK AND SHARES OF TWO SHILLINGS EACH.

This is to Certify that Edward Lawrence Ward *deceased* and Henry John Lewis both of The Cheltenham and Gloucester Building Society, 18, Clarence Street, Cheltenham is the Registered Proprietor of ———— Twenty five ———— Pounds Shillings Stock, fully paid, in THE CHERSONESE (F.M.S.) ESTATES, LIMITED, subject to the Memorandum and Articles of Association of the said Company.

Given under the Common Seal of the Company, this 15th day of September, 1937.

Arthur J. Wardlaw. DIRECTOR

p.p. THOMAS BARLOW & BRO. SECRETARIES.

NOTE. No Transfer of any portion of the Stock comprised in this Certificate will be registered until this Certificate has been delivered at the Company's Registered Office, 49-51 Eastcheap, London E.C.3

THE STOCK IS TRANSFERABLE IN AMOUNTS AND MULTIPLES OF 2/-.

TRANSFER OFFICE, 5, SPENCER PARADE, NORTHAMPTON.

DEPOSIT ACCOUNT BOOK

CLOSED A/C.

M.K. ALFRED J. LANCE
No. 73509 M.B.

CHELTENHAM & GLOUCESTER BUILDING SOCIETY,
Clarence Street, CHELTENHAM.

J. R. MILLICAN.
General Manager and Secretary.

Edward Lawrence Ward founded the department store in his name in 1901. By 1921 the store occupied extensive premises on the corner of North Street and the High Street. At this time, the Ward family lived at Battledown and Edward was a trustee of the estate and a churchwarden of Holy Apostles' Church. The Wards moved out of Cheltenham, returning by the 1930s to live in Hatherley Court Road. Edward was Mayor of Cheltenham between 1933 and 1935, and in 1935, he became President of the Cheltenham & Gloucester Building Society, which then had assets of over £6 million and 50,000 accounts (see Share Certificate from 1937 above). In 1951 Edward was President and Chairman of the Society. Sadly, he died in 1953. Many will remember the Cheltenham District Office in Clarence Street, illustrated on the cover of the Deposit Account Book, before extensive redevelopment of the site in the 1970s.

St Mary's Mission children with Miss Choate, *c.* 1932. Les Cummings and his brother Fred were regular attendees at the mission hall from the age of about five. Miss G.M. Choate, always remembered for her white lace collars, conducted the mission, coaching and arranging performances with the children. St Mary's Mission Hall is now more commonly known as 'the old chapel' in 'the gardens'. The chapel was built in 1831 as the New Burial Chapel to serve the new burial ground, which was in use between 1831 and 1864, until the cemetery at Bouncer's Lane, Prior's Road, was opened. The 'old cemetery' was cleared and levelled in 1966 and opened to the public as Churchill Gardens.

The wedding of Leslie Kenneth Cummings and Joyce Edna Beatrice Gibbons at St Mary's Parish Church on 23 August 1952. The best man was Albert Tibbles, the bridesmaids were Jean Gibbons, Barbara Gibbons and Doreen Gibbons, photographs by Allaways, flowers by Cyphers, dresses from Peter Robinson, the bride's veil from Madame Beatrice Taylor and jewellery by Edgar Mann the Jewellers. Les and Joyce both grew up in the St Paul's area of Cheltenham and met as teenagers. In 2002 they celebrated their Golden Wedding Anniversary.

Above: The Town Hall was built in 1903. Photographs such as this one by E.M. Bailey of the lavish interior decoration of the Main Hall, with its marble pillars and decorative ferns, were soon reproduced as postcards. This card was posted in 1904. The building was designed by Gloucester architect Frederick Waller.

Above: Tea dances were a regular feature of the Town Hall Programme until quite recently. This lucky lad escorted two lovely lassies in fancy dress to the Children's Tea Dance at the Town Hall, *c.* 1933. Doreen Newman is holding a parasol in her right hand and her brother Ken's hand with her left. Amina Chatwin is the other little girl. Amina's mother, Phyllis Elston, had studios in Wellington Street. These dances, always held at Christmas and Easter, became a tradition for many Cheltenham families.

Right: Concerts continued throughout the war. Cheltenham had large numbers of servicemen in the town wanting rest and relaxation and seeking to be entertained. This programme of a concert at the Town Hall given by the Cheltenham Spa Orchestra is from April 1940.

Opposite below: The Town Hall has always been a popular venue for dinners and functions. This photograph is from 1938. Note the flowers and ferns on the tables and the numerous plants in pots on the floor.

TOWN HALL

Entertainments Manager: G. A. M. Wilkinson

Cheltenham Spa Orchestra

Directed by ARTHUR COLE
Leader: Frederick Parrington

Sunday Evening.   14th April, 1940
7-30 p.m.

1—Spanish Gipsy Dance _____ _____ _____ Mowery

2—Intermezzo _____ "Shy Serenade" _____ Scott Wood
(by request)

3—Melodies from the film "The King Steps Out" Kreisler

4—Medley of favourite waltzes _____ _____ arr. Winter

5—CARL CARLISLE—"An Evening with the Stars"

6—Selection _____ "Cavalcade" _____ Noel Coward
(by request)

7—Entr'actes (a) "Mitzi" _____ _____ Bridgmont
(b) "The Gipsy Fiddler" _____ Engleman
(Solo Violin Frederick Parrington)

8—Song Intermezzo "Roses of Picardy" _____ Haydn Wood
(by request)

9—Three modern tunes
"There'll Always be an England" (Vocalist Ron Bowles)
"My Lady" (Vocalist George Macdowell)
and "Good Morning" from "Babes in Arms"

10—CARL CARLISLE

11—One Step _____ "Signorina" _____ Bianco

NATIONAL ANTHEM

PROGRAMME   1D.   BURN'S PRESS

Early literature advertising the Town Hall stressed its 'unique advantages': the Conference Hall seating 2,000 and reception rooms, lounge, offices, all on one floor, and connected by covered way with the Winter Garden. This view from 1929 clearly shows the proximity of the Town Hall and Winter Garden.

'CIRCUS TODAY' is advertised at the Winter Garden on this card posted in January 1930. The Winter Garden (or Cheltenham's Crystal Palace as it was known) opened in 1878, designed by a local architect J.T. Darby. It served a variety of uses: concert hall, roller-skating rink, for bazaars, exhibitions and all kinds of functions. But the acoustics were far from perfect and the building was said to be incredibly draughty. In 1885, the Winter Garden was converted temporarily for three months into an amphitheatre for John Sanger's circus. Subsequently, the building was frequently used by travelling circuses.

WINTER GARDEN,
CHELTENHAM.

Telephone: CHELTENHAM 512

Monday, June 22nd.   For One Week Only.

Daily at 2.30, 5.15 and 8 p.m.
NOT CONTINUOUS.   SEATS MAY BE RESERVED.

A BIG SUPER PRODUCTION

THE EPIC OF EVEREST

A WONDER FILM OF ADVENTURE ON THE ROOF OF THE WORLD
ILLUSTRATING THE GREAT EXPEDITION FOR THE
CONQUEST OF MOUNT EVEREST IN 1924

The Most Sensational and Daring Effort to secure a Picture ever made, photographed by

Capt. J. B. NOEL, F.R.G.S.,
who will appear at each performance.

What the Newspapers say:

WEEKLY DISPATCH   "A chapter of Screen Sensations hitherto unequalled."

DAILY MAIL . . . "More adventure. No colours of novels could be more interesting than Capt. Noel's film."

DAILY EXPRESS . . "A sweeping triumph of British Cinematography."

SUNDAY HERALD . . "Will creep the Screens of the country, and of the world."

SEVEN LAMAS

BROUGHT BACK BY CAPT. NOEL FROM THE INTERIOR OF TIBET WILL BE
SEEN AT THE WINTER GARDEN DURING THE WHOLE OF THE WEEK AND
GIVE A SHORT PERFORMANCE PRIOR TO THE SHOWING OF THE FILM.
THIS IS THE FIRST TIME IN THE HISTORY OF THE WORLD THAT A LAMA
HAS SET FOOT IN A EUROPEAN COUNTRY.

The Whole Performance will be the same as presented for
Eight Weeks at the New Scala Theatre, London.

Films were first shown at the Winter Garden in 1910 and continued through the 1920s. This poster advertises the showing of *The Epic of Everest*, illustrating the Great Expedition for the conquest of Mount Everest in 1924, with the added attraction of seven llamas 'brought back by Capt. Noel from the interior of Tibet' which 'will be seen at the Winter Garden during the whole of the week and give a short performance prior to the showing of the film'!

This photograph was taken shortly after the bandstand was erected in the Gardens. The chairs these two ladies are about to sit in for the concert cost 2d each as can be seen by the ticket shown here. Tickets and this photograph were found in a scrapbook made by the young man taking the photographs in 1920. By 1939, the Winter Garden building had deteriorated to such an extent that it was considered dangerous to the public. Demolition started in 1940. After the war, the site was laid out as the Imperial Gardens. The bandstand was sold in 1948 to Bognor Regis – where it stands today on the seafront.

These young ladies were office staff of Associated Motorways, originally based at the Black & White Motorways' building, which was bombed during the war. After the bombing they were temporarily accommodated at the Red & White Bus Co. offices in Pittville Street (where this photograph was taken). The girls were subsequently re-located back to the bombed site to work in offices over the garage at the back of the site, which had not been damaged. Joyce Sharpe (née Portlock) has remembered some of the girls' names. If you were one of these girls please get in touch with the author. Standing, from left to right: Frances Tyler (née Wheeler), Marion ? (née Smith), Joyce Sharpe (née Portlock), Elizabeth Paish (née Hailing). Seated: -?-, Kay Baglin (née Carter), Phyllis ? (née Jenkins), Ruby ? (née Harvey).

This photograph shows the coach station as it was prior to the bombing in 1940, in which the building at the front, St Margaret's, was destroyed. A new booking hall, waiting room and offices were built in the 1950s. The coach station was closed in 1986. The site, currently used for parking, still waits in 2003, for agreement as to its future use.

Bennington Hall Sunday School group, *c.* 1950. If you were one of the children in either of the photographs on this page or can help to identify them please contact the author. Children identified to date in this group: Gillian Barr, Beryl Grinham, Diane Hircombe, Aileen King, Carol Lewis, Maureen Millard, Janet Orme, Diane Rimell, Lynda Sharpe.

Bennington Hall Sunday School group, *c.* 1955. Identified so far in this group are: Joyce Attwood, Gillian Barr, Sandra Brazil, Beryl Grinham, Diane Hurcome, Jacky Iles, Carol Lewis, Janet Orme, Christine Randall, Jean Ransome, Lynda Sharpe, Judith Townsend.

The Cheltenham Ambulance pictured here was presented to the town by Cheltenham Motor Club. This photograph was taken on the former Athletic Ground where motorcycle football was popular from the 1920s. 'Pip' Draper is standing by the ambulance fourth from left. Howard Locke is standing third from the right and his brother Cecil is kneeling far left.

Staff and their families of Steels Garage, pictured in Albion Street in the early 1950s before setting off on an outing, believed to be to London. Jean Bint (née Scriven) is in the group with her parents Albert and Maud Scriven. Albert, pictured kneeling third from left, joined Steels upon leaving school and spent his entire working life, apart from war service, as an electrical engineer there, retiring in 1970.

Many readers will have travelled to school on Kearsey's coaches and will no doubt remember the coloured tickets – this one was mauve with 3d stamped in green.

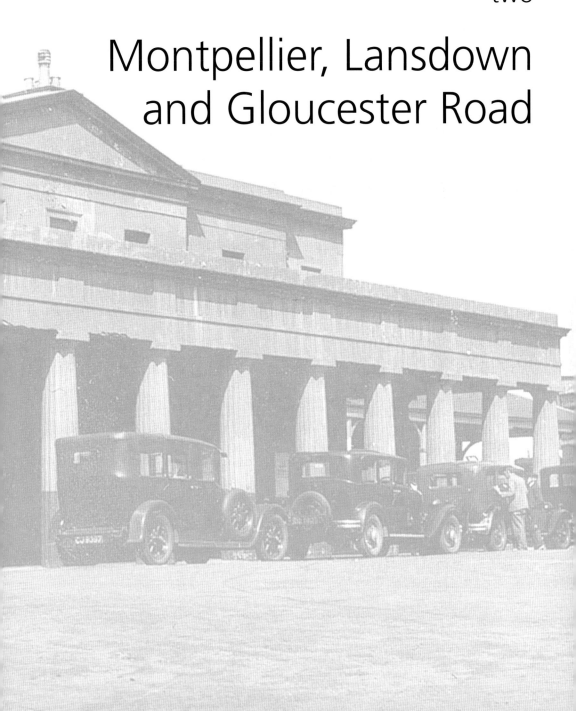

two

Montpellier, Lansdown and Gloucester Road

Above: The Queen's Hotel has stood at the top of the Promenade and at the gateway to Montpellier since it opened in 1838. This grand hotel was not an instant success and in 1852 it was sold for a mere fifth of its original cost of £47,000. However, it has remained a showpiece for Cheltenham over the years and has attracted a glittering array of notables and celebrities, including many royals. In 1900, The Automobile Club's 1,000-mile trial came through Cheltenham and the eighty-three entrants parked in the Gardens and had lunch at the Queen's Hotel. Sir Charles Rolls recorded the fastest time of 37.63mph in this event. A copy of this postcard, produced at the 'Looker-On' Printing Works, was posted in 1913. The Queen's Hotel was, at this time, the official quarters of the Royal Automobile Club, the Motor Union and the Automobile Association. It advertised 'Garage 50 cars/Pits/Repairs'. Two 3-digit telephone numbers were given in the advertisement: 913 & 914.

No. 2 Queen's Circus was built in 1838 and was used continuously as a tea and grocery shop until 1985. C.J. Morgan & Co. pictured here in around 1900 took over the business in 1872 and ran it for the next 113 years.

The Villas and Lansdown Terrace were constructed during the 1830s. Several pairs of villas were planned but they were not all built. Building at Lansdown was hindered by a national banking and financial crisis and Pearson Thompson was forced to sell his interest in the estate to Robert and Charles Jearrad, who greatly altered Papworth's original plan.

Opposite below: Archery was an accepted social activity for the leisured classes in the 1850s. The National Archery Meeting was held in Cheltenham in 1856 and the Montpellier Archery Grounds were advertised as 'open daily, from Ten to Dusk, for parties desirous of learning this beautiful Art'. The Cheltenham Archery Club held its first competitive meeting at Montpellier on 27 June 1857. Archery continued in the gardens until the 1930s. This photograph is another by E.M. Bailey taken prior to the First World War. The method of target construction here is of interest. It is thought the bosses were almost certainly made and sold by Friskneys of Cheltenham, operating from 23 Pittville Street in 1902.

This Burrows postcard was posted in Cheltenham on 12 February 1906 and stamped 11.30 a.m. The sender of the card writes to tell Mrs Walsh of 3 Rodney Place: 'very sorry, hoped to have seen you today but am going by motor to Cleeve and have to go out to tea afterwards'. It is probable that the card would have been delivered to Mrs Walsh before 3 p.m. the same day! The Gordon Lamp, in the centre of Lansdown Road, was lit for the first time in 1887. It was converted to electricity in 1900. The Glo'ster House Private Hotel can be seen to the right.

Glo'ster House Private Hotel,
————LANSDOWN,————

Loftiest and Best Position in Cheltenham.

South Aspect. . Electric Light throughout.
Well-appointed Bath Rooms.   Corporation Sanitary Certificate.

MOTOR AND CYCLE ACCOMMODATION.

A well-appointed Lounge.

Telephone **836**   J. T. IRELAND, Proprietor.

The Glo'ster House Private Hotel claimed the 'loftiest and best position in Cheltenham', offered motor and cycle accommodation and boasted a Corporation Sanitary Certificate. This advertisement appeared in a guidebook, c. 1910.

This view is similar to the one opposite but some significant changes have taken place. The horse and carriage have gone and the motor car has arrived. And the hotel is now The Montpellier Spa Hotel. An early letter card advertising this hotel offers *en pension* terms from 4-6 guineas per week or from 17s 6d per day. All bedrooms were equipped with hot and cold running water, and early morning tea cost 6d.

William Philip Brown, known as Bill, is the boy in the middle of this group pictured trainspotting on Malvern Road Station, *c.* 1933. Bill and the boy on his right both have binoculars. Bill attended the Central School whilst the two older boys sitting on either side of him are wearing Grammar School caps. Bill's maternal grandfather, Tom Phillips, was the miller at Alstone Mill and Tom was born at the mill in 1921. Malvern Road station was constructed to serve the new GWR Honeybourne line. It was one of several stations in Cheltenham to be closed in the 1960s.

Lansdown Station was built in the 1840s. The original pillared frontage was removed in 1961, except for one solitary pillar, which was left standing. The early guidebooks describe Lansdown as a first-class station on the Midland system between Birmingham, Bristol and Bath, thus giving direct communication with all the great towns of the north as well as Bournemouth and all the health resorts of Dorset, Devon and Cornwall. Today, trains leave from Cheltenham Lansdown for all destinations.

Platforms at Lansdown Station, *c.* 1900. In 1993, part of the film *The Whistle Blower*, starring Michael Caine, was shot at Lansdown Station.

Readers who remember the 1930s will know that Gloucestershire had reason to be proud of a particular train. The 2.30 express from Cheltenham became known as the Cheltenham Flyer and earned the title of 'the fastest train in the world', beating the record held in 1931 by the Canadian Pacific Railway. On 6 June 1932, hauled by the 4-6-0 *Tregenna Castle*, it took just under fifty-seven minutes to travel from Swindon to Paddington, which meant it had travelled at an average speed of almost 82mph; 91mph was recorded between Reading and Twyford. Approximately 25cwts of coal and 3,000 gallons of water were used on the Swindon–Paddington run.

This postcard, posted in the 1930s, shows the MR No. 35 leaving Cheltenham. Interestingly, the card was sent 'with the Season's Greetings' to J.N. Maskelyne Esq. at 4 Woburn Square WC1. J.N.M. or 'Jack' was the grandson of John Nevil Maskelyne, the famous Victorian illusionist, born in Cheltenham in 1839. Jack was an engineer and a keen railway enthusiast, and wrote and illustrated several books on railways. As a child he helped his father Nevil and his grandfather make models of stage sets and 'magical apparatus' for their stage shows.

BRITISH RAILWAYS

PASSENGER TRAIN ALTERATIONS

26th OCTOBER to 7th DECEMBER inclusive, 1958
and
11th JANUARY to 1st MARCH inclusive, 1959

OWING TO

ENGINEERING WORK

between

CHELTENHAM

and

GLOUCESTER

PASSENGER TRAINS

between

LONDON AND CHELTENHAM SPA

also

**THE NORTH OF ENGLAND,
WOLVERHAMPTON, BIRMINGHAM**

and

SOUTH WALES AND THE WEST OF ENGLAND

shewn herein will run at altered times.

OCTOBER, 1958.

Left: Some things never change! In 1958-9 some trains from Cheltenham were either cancelled or their times amended due to engineering work between Cheltenham and Gloucester. Buses were laid on in some instances but the leaflet clearly states that 'heavy luggage, perambulators, cycles, etc. will not be conveyed on any of the special bus services'.

Below: This undated card, believed to be staff of H.H. Martyn & Co. at the Sunningend Works, Lansdown, was addressed to Mr W.V. Bliss at No.1 Rose Cottage, Alstone Lane, Cheltenham. On the card is written 'third left bottom row Mr Bliss'.

H.H. Martyn & Co.'s Sunningend Works, Lansdown, from the air. H.H. Martyn was founded in 1888. The firm took over the site in Lansdown, formerly used by the Trusty Engine Works and Letheren's Vulcan Iron Works, renaming it Sunningend. In the 1920s, more than 1,000 highly skilled craftsmen were employed at the Sunningend Works. Their craftsmanship can still be seen today all over the world, including such items as The Cenotaph in Whitehall and the Speaker's Chair in the House of Commons. H.H. Martyn's closed in 1972. In 1917, the famous Gloucestershire Aircraft Co. Ltd was formed and also operated at Sunningend, employing 780 staff and producing 45 aircraft a week in 1918. The aerodrome used by GAC Ltd was at Brockworth.

In 1926, The Gloucestershire Aircraft Co. Ltd changed its name to The Gloster Aircraft Co. Ltd because of the difficulties foreign companies had with the spelling of Gloucestershire. The move to Hucclecote started in 1925 and was completed by 1930. The illustration shows correspondence from Sunningend in 1926 overstamped with the word Gloster.

Aerial view of the Gas Works with the Gloucester and Tewkesbury roads clearly visible. In 1815-6 the Cheltenham Gas Manufactory was established on the Tewkesbury Road. Tesco's superstore now stands on part of the site. Readers will recognise the former Gas Offices building, which has been retained in the development, at the bottom of the photograph, where Gloucester Road meets the High Street.

The gasholders in Gloucester Road. The height of the pedestrians in contrast with the sheer enormity of these holders gives an indication of their size. What the residents felt when these were first erected one can only imagine!

Right: The new Ambulance Headquarters in Gloucester Road were officially opened on 27 June 1937 with a service held in a marquee. The Lecture Hall cost £2,200 and the garage £350, all funds having been raised by the people of Cheltenham. In 1936, the total number of casualties transported was 1,124, of whom 174 were said to be street casualties. At this time, three paid first-aid drivers were employed, all other duties being carried out by voluntary staff. Ambulances in service were: the Agg-Gardner Memorial Ambulance, the Cheltenham Motor Club Ambulance, the Cheltenham Racecourse Ambulance (used in an emergency) and a private Saloon Ambulance. In 1937, the New Motor Ambulance was purchased to replace the Agg-Gardner Memorial Ambulance, with funds from the Sir James Agg-Gardner Memorial Trust and the Coronation Ambulance Fund, and £175 still needing to be raised.

Below: Ambulance staff, *c.* 1938.

THE
Official Opening Ceremony

OF THE

CHELTENHAM AMBULANCE HEADQUARTERS

(GLOUCESTER ROAD)

BY

HIS WORSHIP THE MAYOR OF CHELTENHAM
(Councillor D. L. Lipson, M.A., C.C., M.P.)

ON

SUNDAY, JUNE 27th, 1937,

at 3 p.m.

Gloucester Road Council Schools pre-First World War. Cheltenham's first state-run school opened in Gloucester Road in 1907. In 1914, it became the Central School and later the Technical High School. More recently, the buildings were used by Gloscat and known as the Christchurch Annexe. The Annexe and Gloscat's Park campus were sold to fund the new Gloscat campus in Princess Elizabeth Way. In 2002, despite fervent protests by campaigners anxious to save the building, the old school was demolished and has now been replaced by housing. A plaque marking the fact that the school was used as a hospital during the First World War was saved from the building and is now in the Cheltenham Museum.

Gloucester Road schoolchildren, *c.* 1956

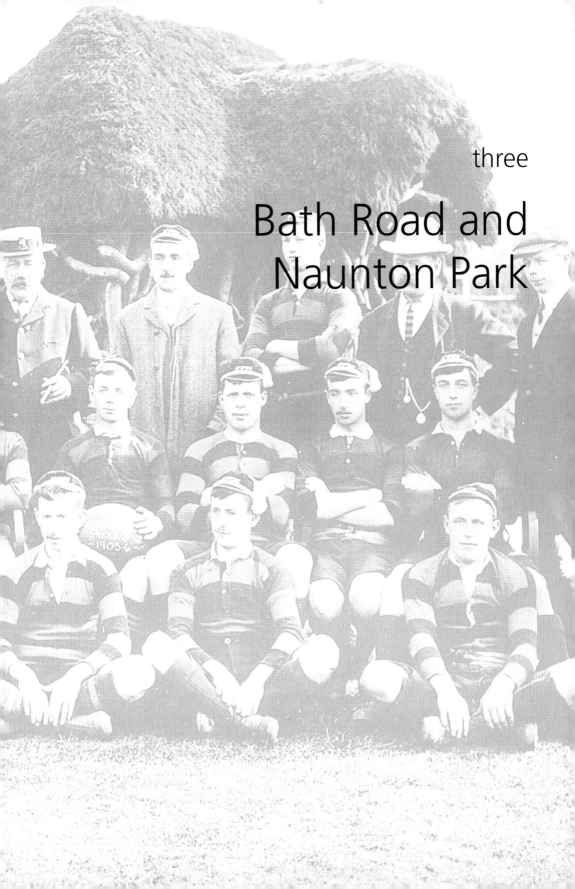

three

Bath Road and
Naunton Park

Cheltenham College was founded in 1841 as a proprietary college, starting life in a house in Bayshill Terrace. The Revd Francis Close, then Rector of Cheltenham, was influential in its founding and one of its Vice-Presidents. In 1843, the College moved to its present site on the Bath Road. Cricket has always been a feature of college life. The Revd T.A. Southwood, the Headmaster of the Military Department appointed in 1843, levelled a piece of land for cricket and taught the boys how to play. In 1847 there is a college cricket match recorded against Birmingham Club, won by the College. Cricket Week was introduced in 1878 and given Festival status in 1906. The Cheltenham Cricket Festival, held every summer on the College grounds, attracts many visitors to the town.

Above: An extract from a partially completed Gloucestershire County Cricket Club Official Score Card for the three-day fixture in August 1927, Gloucestershire *v* New Zealand. Many of the Gloucestershire names will be familiar. The scorecard cost 2d.

Left: A similar scorecard in August 1946 now costing 3d. These were apparently printed on the College Ground by Shenton's Printing Works, Cheltenham. On this occasion, Gloucestershire and India were playing, with familiar names such as W.L. Neale and Goddard in the Gloucestershire side. Spectators for the 1946 season were advised to bring their own refreshments due to the limited supplies available.

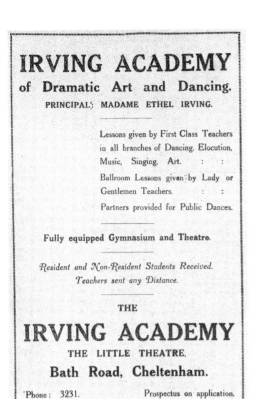

HOUSE OF COMMONS

CHARLES G. IRVING, M.P. Cheltenham Spa, Mayor 1958-60 and 1971-72

Above left: This advertisement for the Irving Academy, run by Madame Ethel Irving, appeared in September 1927, in *The Cheltenham Quarterly*, the official bulletin of the Public Art Gallery & Museum. Madame Irving continued to advertise her School for Girls, Dancing and Dramatic Art, at 105 Bath Road, opposite Cheltenham College, through the 1930s. In 1938, the Hotel Cosyn opened at 105 Bath Road (Mrs E. Irving, proprietess). This was followed by the Irving Hotel, at 105/107 Bath Road, run by the family until the mid-sixties. In 1976, plans were approved to convert the former Irving Hotel into flats and offices.

Above right: Alderman Charles Graham Irving was Mayor of Cheltenham in the 1950s and again in the 1970s and elected Conservative Member of Parliament for Cheltenham in 1974, 1979, 1983 and 1987. He served forty-eight years on the Borough Council and was knighted during Margaret Thatcher's government. He died in 1995. This likeness was drawn by Mr Brian White in 1976. The drawing was then forwarded to Alderman Irving for his approval and signature. Also featured in the drawing is the Cheltenham Coat of Arms, received by the town in 1887, with the motto *Salubritas et Eruditio*, meaning 'Health and Learning'.

Above right: Moorend Dairy, owned by William Frederick Sims, with the horse and cart belonging to the dairy outside, *c.* 1911. The shop stood next to the old Moorend Post Office (248 Bath Road). William lived at the Dairy with his wife Sarah and family until they moved to Crook's Cottages in Pilley, where he died in 1926. His son Thomas continued as a dairyman. In the 1950s, after a succession of owners, the shop passed to Mr William Hicks of Church Farm, who traded as Leckhampton Dairies.

Above left: Leckhampton Dairies Ltd purchased the adjoining property in the Bath Road, in around 1960. The two were combined to produce one store offering a large variety of provisions including wine and spirits. Leckhampton Dairies advertised 'Purity, Service and Satisfaction'. It was a sad day for local residents when this popular shop closed in 1984. The premises later reverted back to two shops.

Left: The original Emmanuel Church stood near the junction of Exmouth Street and Naunton Terrace. It was a corrugated-iron structure, erected in 1872 as a mission hall for St Luke's. In *Kelly's Directory* for 1902 it is described as 'a mission church at the Naunton end of the Parish seating 960 persons'. In the late 1870s, the church suffered severe damage from a heavy fall of snow but, in 1916, fire completely destroyed the building. Worship carried on for many years in an old school room in Naunton Terrace. The new Emmanuel Church was finally built in Fairfield Parade in 1937.

These girls from Emmanuel Sunday School were enjoying a picnic in 1944 on Leckhampton Hill. Included in the group are Pat Parker, Marion Hyde and Yvonne Parsloe. The photograph was taken by Doreen Jewell (née Newman). Doreen was a Sunday School teacher at Emmanuel during the 1940s and '50s.

1955 is thought to be the date of this Emmanuel Sunday School Christmas party. Linda Jewell is in the front row holding David Sully. The party was held in the old Emmanuel Church hall, now demolished and replaced by housing.

Emmanuel United Football Club, 1911. The picture was taken by the photographer from the
St Paul's area of Cheltenham, Harold T. Stokes. On the back of the card is written 'with love
G.F. Bullock'. Apart from this no identification has been possible. If you can help, please contact
the author.

The date on the rugby ball is 1905-6. The Naunton Park team is standing on the Naunton Park
Ground in front of the old thatched bandstand, which was erected in the late 1890s, and funded
by Mrs St Clair Ford in memory of her late husband. In 1903, the Council paid £12 for material
to re-thatch the bandstand. In 1925, the condition of the bandstand had deteriorated so much that
it was removed. Naunton Park played from 1899 to 1954 (from 1932 as Naunton Park Old
Boys). Their colours were green on black hoops and their headquarters was the former
Leckhampton Inn. J.D. Bendall is recognisable in the back row, second from left. John David
Bendall is listed in the *Who's Who in Cheltenham* in 1911 as 'a Town Councillor representing the
South Ward on the Corporation. Home Orchard, Leckhampton'. He was subsequently Mayor for
Cheltenham, from 1918 to 1921.

The Providence Baptist Chapel in Naunton Parade opened in 1870. Former Sunday School children have fond memories of Mr Salmon, Superintendent in the 1930s, and Mrs Salmon, his wife. They are pictured at the back left on this photograph taken around 1930 on a summer treat to Cranham. These annual treats were eagerly looked forward to by the children. Included in this group are Doreen and Ken Newman, Win and Beatrice Furley, and Beryl Marshall.

Naunton Park Infants Class II, *c.* 1930. Seated at front, from left to right: -?-, Geoff Edwards, Peter Sutton, -?-, Len (Chubb) Jewell, -?-. Second row: Joan Whiting, -?-, Joy Woolley, Joyce Cripps, Doreen Newman, -?-, Iris Bennett, Sybil Toms. Third row: Joan Hall, -?-, Dorothy Jelfs, John Moxey, Ursula Poulton, Margaret Wilson, -?-, Muriel Ballinger. Back row: Peter Corbett, -?-, Derek Bennett, -?-, -?-, Billy Boulton, -?-, Leonard Spiller. Naunton Park Schools opened in 1907, one of the first state schools to open in the town. In 1930, the girls' school became a mixed primary school, which it still is today.

Naunton Park Juniors Class I, *c.* 1933. Seated at front, from left to right: –?–, 'Snowy' Pearson, Roy Parr, Ivor Putnam, George Powis. Second row: Doreen Newman, Irene Gardner, Joan Whiting, Nellie Jeanes, Eva Welch, Brenda Gardner, Pat Tyler, Joyce Payton, –?–, Sybil Toms, Joyce Pritchard, Audrey Long. Third row: –?–, Joan Cox, Jean Smith, Joyce Dent, Jean Goatman, Doris Greenwood, –?–, Mary Gillett, Marie Roach, Alma West, Doreen Turner. Back row: Tony Potts, –?–, John Noble, Derek Bennett, Peter Townsend, –?–, –?–, Martyn Law, David Herzig.

Naunton Park Rugby XV 1954 with Mr Whittaker, sports master. John Smith provided this photograph which is signed by eleven of the team on the reverse. Standing, from left to right: John Smith, Trevor Edwards, –?–, D. Smith, R. Trainer, Eddy Whistler, Billy Beaumont. Seated: Mr Whittaker, R. Harris, John Elston, Peter Tapsell, –?–, Brian Howe, ? Freeman. Kneeling: Chris Bridges, D. Williams.

Naunton Park Hockey Team 1957. Front row, from left to right: Patricia Webb, Diana Summers, Diane Walton, Pauline ?, Maureen Smith, Margaret Bray. Back row: Christine Harris, Rosemary Bullock, Monica Barnett, Mary Godfrey, Catherine Knight. Behind the group the rugby team with Mr Wilson, the Headmaster, can just be seen. The hanging sign indicates that a library is available from Monday to Thursday, 6.30 to 8 p.m. Naunton Park was originally built as separate boys' and girls' schools. The two were amalgamated in 1930 and Naunton Park Senior Council School was formed, later becoming Naunton Park Secondary Modern School. The school closed in July 1984.

Naunton Park Juniors. Paul Bishop, Pauline Gilbert, Linda Jewell, Irene Popiel, Bridget Paish and Christine Reed are included in this class photograph taken in around 1961. Can you name the rest of the group?

The maypole dancing and the school group on this page are from the author's days at Naunton Park Junior School. Maypole dancing and country dancing were practiced on the 'rec'. Hay Cottage Homes, built in 1899, can be seen in the background.

Classes of around forty were quite common in the late 1950s and uniform was normally strictly adhered to. The Naunton Park uniform was quite distinctive in navy and gold. Approximately forty-five years after this photograph was taken, six of the girls (circled) met up, and found plenty to talk about!

Still recognisable after all these years! The girls met in October 2002 and school seemed like only yesterday. From left to right: Carol Hartley (née Fruin), Elaine Heasman (née Worsfold), Elizabeth Taylor (née Turner), Marian Lewis (née Tiller), Pauline Higgs (née Weeks) and Pat Turner (née Barnes).

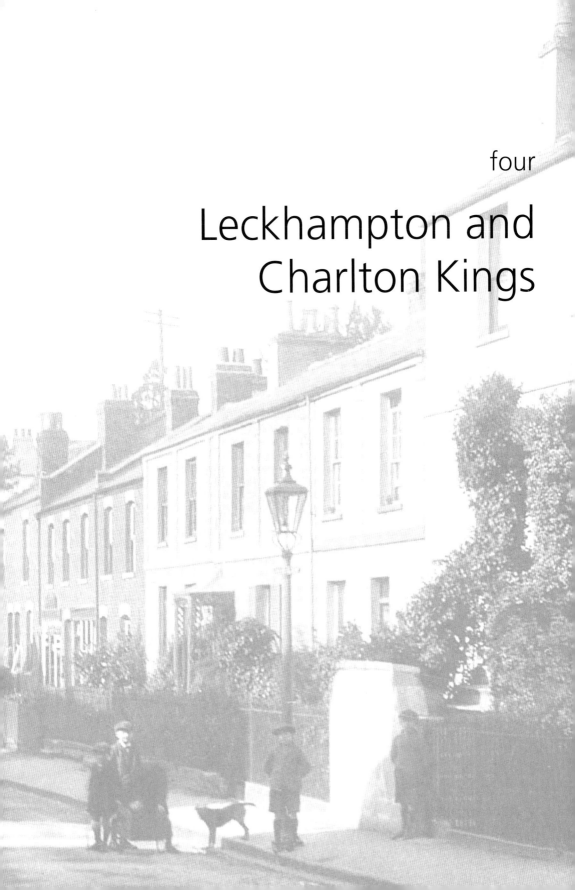

four

Leckhampton and Charlton Kings

This is the regular service to the Malvern Inn from St James' station via the High Street, *c.* 1900. The omnibus carried plenty of advertising even in these early days. The conductor is believed to be Mr J. Birt of Short Street (b.1882) and on top of the omnibus, left to right: –?–, Fred Birt (b.1874), Mr Siddall, Mr Locke (baker), Bernard George Thompson (Headmaster of Leckhampton School for more than twenty years), –?–, Mr Thompson (the schoolmaster's brother), –?–. Mrs Letitia Miriam Kirkham is listed in 1902 as a beer retailer, Leckhampton Road. In recent years, the Malvern Inn has been converted into a private house and now looks very similar to the picture here.

The Leckhampton Motor Service, owned by Mr Victor Nicholls, stood on the corner of Pilley Lane and Leckhampton Road. It was rebuilt in the 1930s. Note the tall row of Shell petrol pumps. Mr Nicholls' son, Austin, learnt his early ironworking skills in his father's garage, becoming a member of the British Guild of Craftsmen. In the 1960s he owned a forge at Lower Swell. Austin died in May 2001. Victor Nicholls' younger son, Norman, is living in Australia and provided this photograph.

Victory celebrations in 1945. Children from Southern Road and Pilford Road line up in fancy dress on 15 August 1945. Terry Enoch, (the tall lad on the right) has identified the following: Ann Bawden, John Cole, his sister Valerie Enoch, Colin Gomersall, Rachel Holyoake, Faye Macfarlane, Robin Roebuck, Jennifer and Jeremy Seavers and Colin Wainwright. The car, a 1938 Hudson Terraplane two-door convertible, belonged to Mr Wood of Southern Road.

This real photographic postcard posted in 1931 provides a clear view of Leckhampton Hill and Blackhedge Farm, lying below Salterley Grange. The evidence of quarrying is clearly visible. In April 2003, a fire took control on the hill for several hours and forty acres of bracken and grassland were destroyed. The hill has been designated a site of Special Scientific Interest and is classed as an area of outstanding natural beauty in the Cotswolds, or 'picturesque' as described on the card.

Left: Charles George Capper, *c.* 1895. He was born in 1875 in Moorend Street and was the grandfather of Geoff Capper who grew up in Leckhampton. Geoff died in 1999, leaving photographs and ephemera to Leckhampton Local History Society and also to the author.

Below: Another view of the hill. This is Cooper's Hill with Green Street below. The house in the foreground has been marked by hand 'The Corner House'.

A deer roast at Southfield Manor, Sandy Lane, in the 1950s. In the photograph are Mr and Mrs Arthur Gardner, then living at the manor, and their guests, including Mr Gershom Wood senior and Mr Wilf Davey. Part of the manor buildings are thought to date from the late seventeenth century.

These stocks date from 1763 and were used for punishing minor offenders. The fear of ridicule was no doubt an effective deterrent. They were originally sited outside the south porch of St Mary's Church and then later moved to behind the village pump. The pump and stocks were both removed in around 1918. Fortunately, the stocks were saved and erected outside the Parish Centre in New Street. A shelter was made to protect them.

Cudnall Street photographed by F.C. Pearce, Cheltenham (spelt CUDALL on the card). Cudnall, meaning Cudda's Hill, was part of an early settlement in Charlton Kings, probably prior to the eleventh century. Before the present top road (now part of the A40) was built, Cudnall Street formed part of an ancient route to London and was still known as London Road in 1884, and Old London Road in 1897.

Langton Grove Road, a cul-de-sac off the London Road, pictured on a card posted in 1911. The house on the left was relatively new when the card was produced. It is still there today, looking very similar but with a more open aspect and a very pretty garden. The building at the bottom of the road is no longer there.

This view of Ryeworth Road, looking towards the Ryeworth Inn, was captured by E.M. Bailey, probably pre-First War. Ryeworth, 'the rye inclosure and farm', was another early settlement in Charlton Kings. The road was cut across Ryeworth Field, *c.* 1770.

A very different view of Ryeworth Road taken after a deep snowfall in the 1980s. The photograph does, however, give an indication of the varied types of housing to be found in this now popular residential road.

This view is of Charlton Hill taken from the Cirencester Road, with Bradley Road off to the left, leading to Garden Road. Bradley Road was so called, in 1933, after its builders E.H. Bradley & Son. Above the junction onto the Cirencester Road is the garage (Station Garage in the 1930s), and beyond that the public house, then the New Inn, which in later years was renamed The Little Owl after the 1981 Cheltenham Gold Cup winner. On the right-hand side behind the trees and railings is Glenure Court, now in flats. This large house started life as two cottages but was rebuilt in 1820 as one dwelling, called Brunswick House, and later renamed Glenure.

The Cotswold Hounds at the Lilleybrook Hotel in the early 1900s, by G.A. Powell, Photo, Cheltenham. Mr Herbert Owen Lord, was a Cotswold man and lived at Lilley. He was Master of the Hunt for fifteen seasons, from 1904 to 1919. Mr Lord kept going throughout the First World War, although the pack had then to be reduced to twenty-five couple.

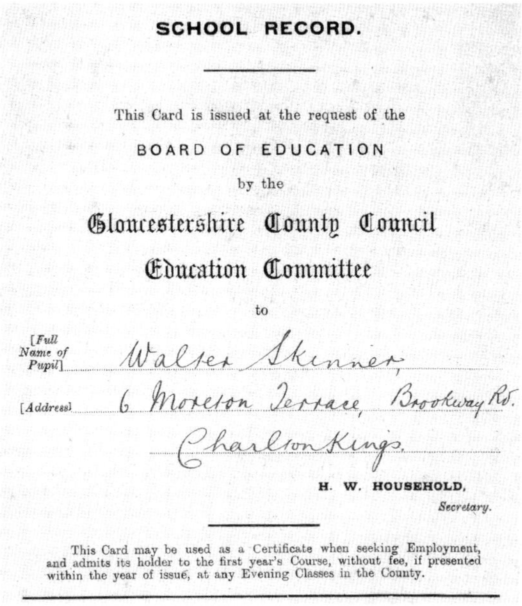

SCHOOL RECORD.

This Card is issued at the request of the

BOARD OF EDUCATION

by the

Gloucestershire County Council

Education Committee

to

[Full Name of Pupil] *Walter Skinner,*

[Address] *6 Moreton Terrace, Brookway Rd.*
Charlton Kings.

H. W. HOUSEHOLD,
Secretary.

This Card may be used as a Certificate when seeking Employment, and admits its holder to the first year's Course, without fee, if presented within the year of issue, at any Evening Classes in the County.

A school record issued in 1920 to Walter Skinner, which he could use as a certificate when seeking employment, or to admit him, free of charge within one year, to any evening class held in the county. Walter had attended Charlton Kings Council School. He was fourteen years and two months old when he left school and the Head Teacher Mr F.J. Fry wrote, 'Conduct excellent. Has worked well.'

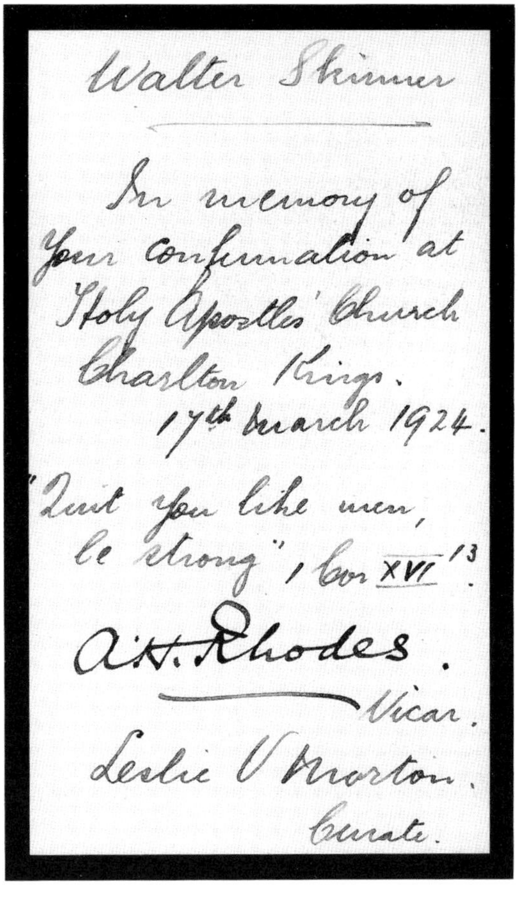

Walter Skinner

In memory of Your confirmation at Holy Apostles' Church Charlton Kings.
17th March 1924.
"Quit you like men, be strong" 1 Cor XVI 13

A.H. Rhodes.
Vicar.
Leslie V Morton.
Curate.

Walter Skinner was confirmed at Holy Apostles Church on 17 March 1924. He received *A Manual of Devotions*, inscribed as shown here.

Above and below: Boys at Charlton Kings Church School, *c.* 1910. Can you help with the accurate dating of these photographs and the identification of the children?

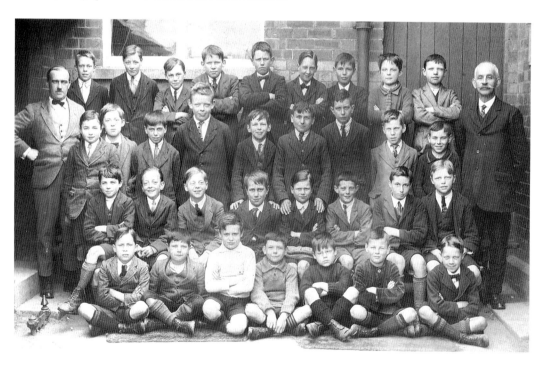

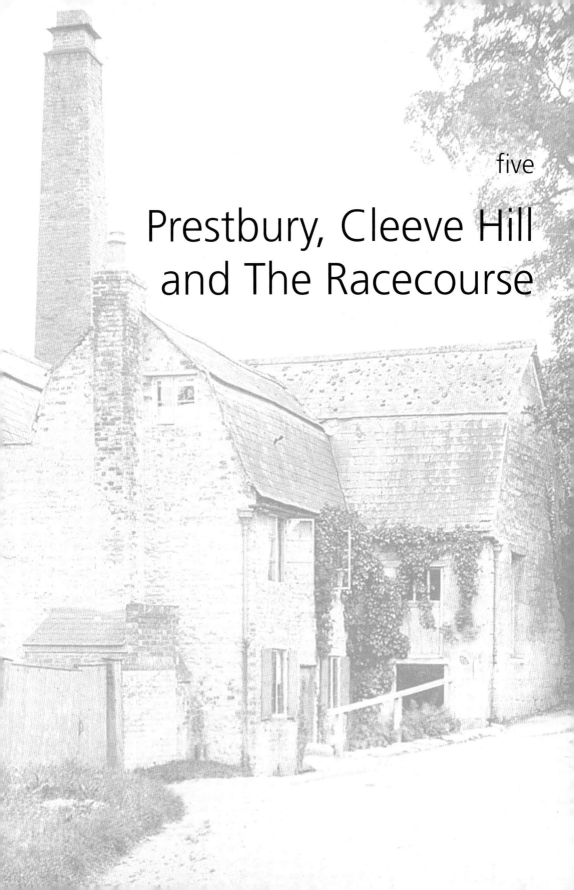

five

Prestbury, Cleeve Hill and The Racecourse

Five roads converge onto this junction known to local people as 'The Weighbridge': Prestbury Road, Bouncer's Lane, Blacksmith's Lane, Deep Street and New Barn Lane. The weighbridge was at the junction of Prestbury Road and Bouncer's Lane. One Prestbury resident remembers the two houses – one being the office and the other belonging to the man who ran the weighbridge – being knocked down when the road was widened. The Women's Institute Hall was built on this corner shortly before the Second World War. Quite an idyllic scene here around 1910 – the children stand in the roadway in no apparent danger.

A different view of the junction to that of the previous picture. The scene is a little less rural with the advent of the motor car and the traffic bollards. The two girls walk up Bouncer's Lane past Randall's Cottage. Bouncer's Gate is mentioned as early as 1617 as one of the boundary points of the Cheltenham Hundred. In the 1820s, the name Bouncer's Lane applied from Prestbury to Charlton Park. The extent of Bouncer's Lane was shortened when Hale's Road was made up in 1846 and further reduced when Cemetery Road was named (now Prior's Road). Randall's Cottage has recently undergone extensive renovation.

An early card of Fourways in Bowbridge Lane seen from the Burgage, formerly Burgage Street and once the main street of Prestbury. The original weekly market and annual fair granted in 1249 by Henry III were believed to have been held here. Fourways used to be two cottages rented by a cordwainer and a yeoman, with a rent of 'five shillings and a peppercorn'.

Published by S.Y. Griffith & Co. in 1826, this engraving is of Field House, described as 'an establishment for young ladies conducted by the Miss Ashwins'. There were many small private schools in the early nineteenth century both in and around Cheltenham. Field House, later known as The Lindens, is situated at the corner of New Barn Lane and The Burgage.

Prestbury used to boast several mills. Lower Mill in Mill Street went out of use towards the end of the nineteenth century and in the 1920s it was used as a laundry. The chimney was subsequently removed and the building converted to a private house. Although some renovation and rebuilding has taken place this view remains similar to this day – even the railing along the side of the road has survived.

Another in a series of postcards by F.E. Pearce. This one of Shaw Green Lane was posted in 1937. This road is an ancient one, leading from the former manor house in Spring Lane to the hilltop pastures. The Parish Pound was situated in Shaw Green Lane. Although some houses are older, much of the residential development began in the first few years of the twentieth century. It is said that when roadworks were being carried out in 1901 in Shaw Green Lane the skeleton of a man with an arrow in his chest was revealed. This is just one of the many ghostly tales Prestbury is renowned for.

HOLY BAPTISM

NAME E............................

....

BAPTIZED ON........................

And put on the Baptism
Roll of the Sunday School
of St Mary's Prestbury

....

SIGNED..........................
Superintendent

The author was baptised on 3 August 1947 at St Mary's Church by the vicar, the Revd Henry Wilmot Hill, and placed on the Roll of the Sunday School of St Mary's. The Superintendent of the Sunday School in 1947 was Miss Winnington-Ingram, a lady who will, no doubt, be remembered with fondness by many residents. Christened Constance Maud, but known as Maud, she came from a famous family. Her father, one of ten children, was the Venerable Edward Henry Winnington-Ingram MA, formerly Archdeacon of Hereford and Canon Residentiary of Hereford Cathedral, who retired to Prestbury in 1925. An uncle, Arthur Foley Winnington-Ingram, became Bishop of London and Chaplain to the London Rifle Brigade. In 1909, Maud went to St Christopher's College, Blackheath, a newly opened training college for Sunday School Teachers and in 1912 joined the staff at Cheltenham Ladies' College, being responsible for Scripture teaching and preparation for Confirmation.

Miss Winnington-Ingram lived at 'Ribbesford' in Shaw Green Lane. Her father had 'inherited' the family living at Ribbesford in Worcestershire in 1876, becoming Rector of Ribbesford and Vicar of Bewdley. Her childhood had been spent in that part of Worcestershire. She is pictured here in the back garden of 'Ribbesford', Prestbury, with her doves.

Above left: In the 1930s tennis courts were provided by Miss Winnington-Ingram for the residents of Prestbury.

Above right: Miss Elisabeth Nalder was companion to Miss Winnington-Ingram. In 1922, Elisabeth Nalder produced this little book for children, which was published in London and subsequently reprinted. A copy was given to Diana Parker as a child. Diana, now Mrs Stanley, treasures the book today after all these years.

Note the fashionable dress and the child's push-along horse in this photograph, taken in Shaw Green Lane. The lady on the right in this photograph is Mrs Humphries.

A Prestbury Group enjoying a tea party in the open air. What is the occasion?

Very little is known about this event, believed to have been held at the Priory. Diana (née Parker) Stanley's mother is the lady in white, back right.

An Old People's Party held at the Women's Institute Hall. Included in the photograph are Mr and Mrs Parker, Miss Fieldhouse and Mrs Thomas.

Prestbury Brownies, including Diana Parker and Wendy Collins, at Cowley Manor, *c.* 1949. Cowley Manor was a popular place for outings in the 1940s and '50s. Over the years it has changed hands several times. Recently, however, it has been restored to its former glory and in May 2003, Cowley Manor Hotel and Health Spa was voted one of the top hotels in the world.

The author and her sister Geraldine with friends at 83 Bouncer's Lane, *c.* 1951. Back row, from left to right: Geraldine Worsfold, Janet Cox, Ann Thomas, Ann Smith, Susan Blacklock, Geoffrey Thomas. Front row: Elaine Worsfold, Heather Smith.

This group photograph was taken in around 1949. Sunday School parties such as this were held in the former skittle alley of The King's Arms in the High Street, now demolished. Included in the group are Wendy Collins, Jennifer Gooch, Diana Parker, Rosemary Parker and Mr Brown, organist for St Mary's Church.

Cleeve Hill has always been popular with walkers and riders alike. *Above left:* This photograph of the author's younger son Matthew with dog Lucy and friend Mark Stinchcombe was taken on a hot summer's day in the 1970s. From this point, which is reached from Bushcombe Lane, the following are signposted: Longwood Common, Gotherington, Granna Lane and Cleeve Common. *Above right:* The author with dog Pepper pictured in the same location twenty years later. The season is different, the sign is slightly more worse for wear, but the countryside here has changed very little.

This card was produced by Cleeve Hill Café and presumably helped to advertise it. The café could be reached by tram as the picture illustrates. It was built in 1901 and was just one of several cafes and tea-houses on the hill in the early years of the twentieth century.

Ed J. Burrow & Co. Ltd Printers, Cheltenham produced this card, which was posted in 1915. The Cleeve Hill Café is reported to have claimed to be able to cope with 200 visitors at short notice. E.J. Burrow is thought to have invested personally in the café. Certainly, in his Publisher's Foreword to the sixth edition of *The Garden Town* (1910-12) he extols the virtues of the hill. He states, 'The Electric Tramway, which conveys one from the centre of the town nearly to the top of Cleeve Hill, is creating a new Malvern on that breezy shoulder of the Cotteswolds.'

The Geisha Tea Rooms stood high on the hill, commanding superb views and helping to promote Cleeve Hill as 'The Cotswold Health Resort'. The Geisha advertised all-inclusive weekends for 10s 6d. This postcard was sent in 1903.

CHELTENHAM RACES

FIRST RACE 1.0 p.m.   EACH DAY   LAST RACE 3.30 p.m.

DAY EXCURSION BOOKINGS
WEDNESDAY, DECEMBER 31st
and THURSDAY, JANUARY 1st
TO

CHELTENHAM SPA
(LANSDOWN)

FROM	DEPART	RETURN FARES		ARRIVAL ON RETURN
		First Class	Second Class	
	a.m.	s. d.	s. d.	p.m.
PAIGNTON	6 50	47/0	31/3	10 25
TORQUAY	6 56			10 17
TORRE	7 1	} 46/3	} 30/9	10 14
NEWTON ABBOT	7 21	44/3	29/6	9 48
TEIGNMOUTH	7 30	42/9	28/6	9 37
DAWLISH	7 37	42/0	28/0	9 29
EXETER (St. Thomas) §	7* 54	38/9	25/9	*
EXETER (St. David's)	8 3	38/3	25/6	9 5
TAUNTON	8 43	28/6	19/0	8 10
BRIDGWATER	9 0	24/9	16/6	7 50
WESTON-S-MARE (Gen.)	9 27	20/9	13/9	7 23
CLEVEDON (‡)	9 19	19/6	13/0	7 56
YATTON	9 40	18/6	12/3	7 40

Cheltenham Spa (Lansdown) arrive 11.37 a.m. Return (same day) depart 5.12 p.m.

CHANGE AT BRISTOL (TEMPLE MEADS) IN BOTH DIRECTIONS.

NOTES : ‡—Change at Yatton in both directions.
§—On the forward journey passengers change at Bristol (Temple Meads) and proceed at 10.30 a.m.
*—Passengers from Exeter (St. Thomas) alight at Exeter (St. David's) on the return journey.

PASSENGERS WISHING TO TRAVEL DIRECT TO CHELTENHAM (RACECOURSE STATION) SHOULD PROCEED FROM BRISTOL (TEMPLE MEADS) AT 10.30 a.m. AND CHANGE AT GLOUCESTER (EASTGATE), PROCEEDING THENCE FROM GLOUCESTER (CENTRAL) AT 12.0 noon, ARRIVING CHELTENHAM (RACECOURSE STATION) AT 12.30 p.m. ON THE RETURN JOURNEY PASSENGERS DEPART CHELTENHAM (RACECOURSE STATION) AT 4.10 p.m. AND CHANGE AT GLOUCESTER (CENTRAL), PROCEEDING THENCE FROM GLOUCESTER (EASTGATE) AT 5.27 p.m.

Passengers can also proceed to the Racecourse by omnibus from
Cheltenham Spa (Landown) Station.

If the Race Meetings are cancelled and notice is received by the British Transport Commission in time for intending passengers to be advised, the fares paid will be refunded on application.

Children under Three years of age, Free ; Three and under Fourteen years of age, half-fare.

In 1958 Day Excursions were advertised to Cheltenham Races travelling on British Railways (Western region) from as far away as Paignton. Passengers could travel to Cheltenham Spa (Lansdown) Station, and then continue to the Racecourse by omnibus or, if wishing to travel direct to the Racecourse Station, could change at Gloucester for Cheltenham (Racecourse Station). Both options also included changing trains at Bristol. The Racecourse Station was opened in 1912. By 1960, all stations north of Cheltenham Racecourse had closed. In 1976, the last train visited the Racecourse and a new GWR – the Gloucestershire Warwickshire Railway Society – was formed, with the objective of saving the line. On Tuesday, 11 March 2003, a train full of excited racegoers steamed proudly into Cheltenham Racecourse Station, the first train to arrive there since 1976 and the first steam-hauled race train since 1965. It may only have been a 20-mile round trip for these passengers but a success story none the less.

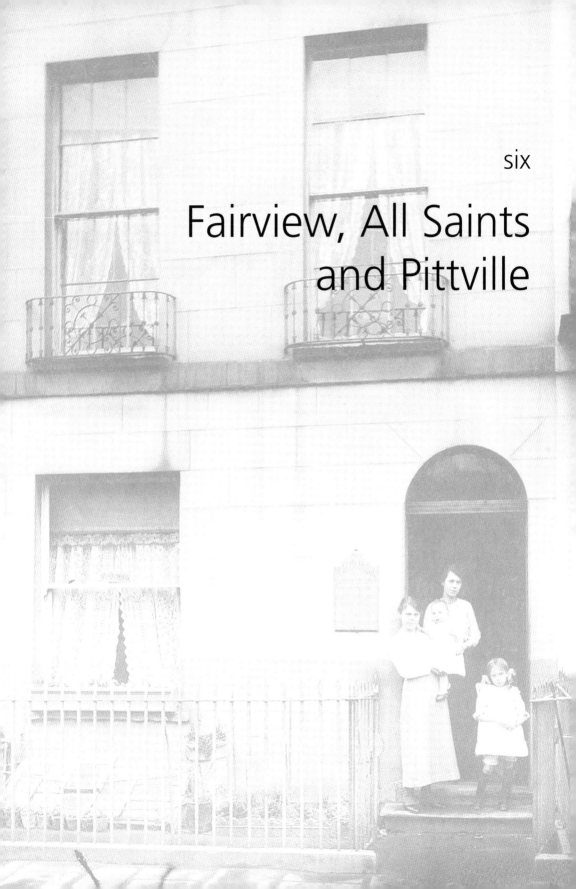

six

Fairview, All Saints
and Pittville

In *Kelly's Directory* of 1902 Edward Eager is listed as a builder, sanitary engineer, plumber and decorator, in Fairview Road. By the time this card was produced a company had been formed and Edward Eager & Co. are described as Contractors for House Decorations. In 1934, Edward Eager & Son are offering '30 years practical experience' and 'House Sanitation and Ventilation executed on the latest Scientific Principles'. The works address is given as 121-123 Fairview Road but advertisements carry the 4-digit phone number of 2938 and the address of 'Silcote', Cranham Road. The family name continued until the 1970s.

Stephens's Grocery & Provision Stores was situated on the corner of Wellington Passage, which, in the 1890s, ran between 95 and 96 High Street and Albion Street.

Richard Brownett was a photographer operating in Hewlett Road from 1876-85, and previously (around 1865) at 45 Duke Street. These small cards, known as *cartes de visites* or calling cards, were very popular before postcards were produced. Regrettably, these cards did not normally carry the name of the subject and, although many have survived, very few portraits can be identified, as is the case here.

Jersey Street is situated off Sherborne Street and building began here in 1825. This photograph was taken in the 1960s, capturing a typical corner shop. Cheltenham had many such shops, most of which have now disappeared and been replaced by 'one-stop shops' or the local supermarket.

Above and below: VE Day 1945 in St James' Street (between the High Street and Albion Street) – adults and children pose for the camera. Keith Smith has identified the following children in the photograph below: Margaret Agg, Marian, Brian, Ken, Beryl and Graham Atkins, Daphne, David and Lawson Bennett, Joyce Birt, Tony Cole, Bert and Eileen Court, Colin and Eric Davies, David Edwards, Albert Fry, Tony Gibbs, Tom Jenkins, Brenda and John Johnson, Russell Jones, Glenda Lane, Maureen and John Newman, Clyde Smith, Keith, Colin, John and Michael Smith, Josie and Jean Smith, John Summers, Melville Underwood, Peter Worthington and Anna Wright. Keith grew up in St James' Street and was born in one of the cottages seen here. These cottages were part of the one side of St James' Street, which was demolished in the 1960s, to make way for a car park.

Above: In 1897, the occupant of 27 North Place is given as Mrs Rachel Clinch, dressmaker. In 1902, William Clinch, carpenter, is listed at this address. Could this be his family outside the house?

Right: The parish of All Saints, Pittville, was formed when boundaries of two neighbouring parishes were adjusted, and because of the activities of a small group anxious to retain a church for High Church, Tractarian worship in the area. The new church was designed by the architect, Mr John Middleton, and was consecrated in 1868. It is built of Cleeve Hill stone with Bath stone dressings. The Calvary was erected in memory of the men from the parish who fell in the First World War, and was dedicated by the Bishop of Gloucester on 10 June 1920.

All Saints Secondary Modern School Athletic Team, winning both girls' and boys' shields for the first time at the inter-schools sports, in the 1950s. The team is pictured on the former Athletic Ground, with Fairview Road in the background, although Keith Smith remembers the sports were held on the College Cinder Track. Keith has identified the following, from left to right, back row: -?-, Valerie ?, Margaret Hooper, Linda Leighton, Sue Lawrence, Keith Smith, Phil Bullock, Ken ?, Hugh Nicholson, Sports Master Ron Upton. Middle row: -?-, Margaret Bailes, Jennifer Wilding, Ann Price, Mike Stancombe, Doug Woodward, Tony Cole, Ron Brislin. Front row: Roger Thorndale, Dennis Humphries, Jimmy Yiend. The school was founded in 1890 and in 1930 became the first senior mixed school in the town. In 1944 it became a secondary modern school but was closed in 1978, and its pupils transferred to other local schools.

Beechurst Avenue off Eldon Road, shortly after building work was completed in 1935. The road was built on land to the rear of the house called Beech Hurst in Hewlett Road and named after it.

A group of students at Christie College, Wellington Road, Pittville, in 1970. A Christie College-trained secretary was to be sought after in the 1960s and '70s.

Opposite below: The Pump Room is a magnificent venue for functions. This is a Scottish Society party celebrating Hogmanay in the 1960s. In the group are: Ken and Monica? Stevens, Hugh Crawford, Doug and Connie Long, Margaret Crawford, Eric and Cynthia Bracey, Pat and Joan Somerville.

This is a more unusual view of the Pump Room showing the semi-circular garden just outside the main entrance. Pittville Estate was the vision of Joseph Pitt MP (1759- 1842). Building began on the Pump Room in 1825 and took about five years to complete. It was the largest of the town's spas. Today, it represents one of Cheltenham's finest 'Regency' buildings and is very popular with both local people and tourists.

This unusual card by Slade Bros. gives the appearance of an aerial view of the launch of the lifeboat *Cheltenham* on Pittville Lake, on 10 October 1866, with the Pump Room in full view. This boat was a Class 38 self-righting prowse 'medium' lifeboat, built in 1866 by Woolfe of Shadwell, 32ft long, 7ft 5in wide and weighing 2 tons. It cost £256 and was paid for by Cheltenham Lifeboat Fund under the leadership of Capt. W. Young RN. It was named *Cheltenham* and served at Burnham on Sea from 1866 to 1887. It was launched on service fourteen times and saved thirty-six lives. After being sold out of service in 1888, it is not known what happened to the *Cheltenham*.

Another lifeboat was launched on Pittville Lake in 1924, although this launch received much less publicity. The weather was disappointing and the day, intended to be a big fundraiser for the RNLI's centenary, was not a financial success.

Another momentous occasion featuring boats on Pittville Lake took place in 1908. The Gloucestershire Historical Pageant was staged in the grounds of Marle Hill House from 6 July to 11 July inclusive, with all profits to the Veterans' Relief Fund. The pageant was in eight episodes, the subject of each episode being explained by a Narrative Chorus, which also sang songs. The chorus represented the rivers and streams of Gloucestershire and were rowed in large boats on the lake. The four principal rivers of the chorus were the Thames, Sabrina, Avona and the Chelt.

The Foundation Stone for the new Pate's Grammar School for Girls, in Albert Road, was laid on 23 July 1938 by Sir Richard Livingstone, President of Corpus Christi College, Oxford, and dedicated by the Lord Bishop of Gloucester. This photograph of the new school was published in the *Cheltenham Chronicle & Graphic* on 23 September 1939. It was reported that the school had opened that week although the building was far from finished. Local girls were now attending school in the mornings and the pupils of King Edward's High School, Birmingham, who had been evacuated to Cheltenham because of the war, were using the building in the afternoons.

These are some of the girls who continued to attend Pate's Grammar School through the war years. Carina Bibby, who provided the photograph, believes it is from 1946. She also remembers that the photograph was taken by Daphne Storey's father. The teacher seated at the front, Miss D.M. Taylor, history mistress, will be familiar to many ex-Pate's girls, as she continued to teach at the school for several years and is remembered by the author in the 1960s. Back row, from left to right: Jean Stokes, Margaret Brown, Joan Wendon, Angela Lewis, Rita Soule, Ray Devall, Marion Halling?. Middle row: Joyce Hewins, Yvonne Nation, Mary Briton, Pat ?, -?-, Ruth Levy, Audrey Faires, Carina Bibby, Effie Smith. Front row: Pamela Giles, Glenys Cunningham, Pat Whitlock, Valerie Williams, Daphne Storey, Margaret Archer, Valerie Whitmarsh-Everis, Norma Halford, Pamela Jones, Honor Larner.

Pate's girls relax at a sports day in the 1960s. Included in the snapshot are: June Hales, Carol Norman, Lyn Rosen, Janet Martin, Moya Job, Susan Hawkins, Jean Barton, Elizabeth Turner, Sandra Skinner, Diane Lawrence, Christine King, Gill Andrews, Tania Hill, June Cangley, Elizabeth McIlroy and Judy Scott.

Some of the girls in the above photograph attended a reunion held in October 2002 at the Old Pats Club in Cheltenham for those who started at Pate's in 1958, in Forms P, Q, R and S. Twenty of those who attended Form S are photographed here, including the author. For some it was the first time they had met since leaving Pate's in the 1960s.

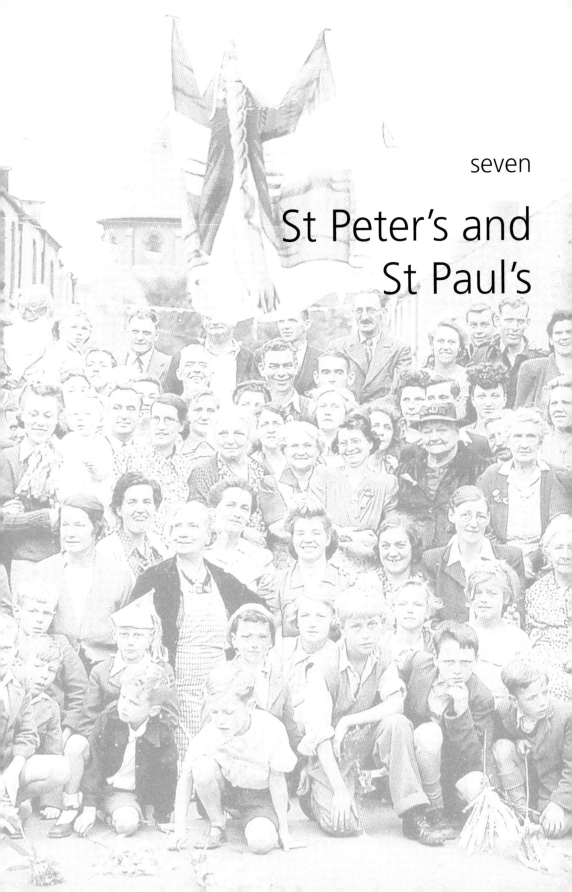

seven

St Peter's and
St Paul's

St Paul's Old Boys RFC on their way to Fromehall Park, Stroud, on 12 November 1921, photographed outside the library buildings in Clarence Street. The sign for St George's Vaults is just visible to the left. The photographer is Harold T. Stokes from nearby St Paul's Road and Dunalley Parade. These 'Old Boys' were former pupils of St Paul's Practising School, located in Swindon Road. The Club played at the Agg-Gardner Recreation Ground from 1896 to 1901 and 1920 to 1922. *The Cheltenham Echo* of the previous day tells us that transport to Stroud would leave at 1.30 p.m. sharp and the team to play against Stroud 'A' (Stroud 2nd XV) was to be selected from the following: F. Morton, R. Griffiths, T. Merrell, E. Taylor, G. Maisey, W. Pearce, E. Brunsden (Capt.), H. Edwards, E. Brooke, F. Midwinter, W. Griffiths, A. Hopkins, H. Wiggell, A. Tannor, H. Williams, A. Fowler. It would be nice to be able to match names and faces. The game was won by the Stroud team 3-0.

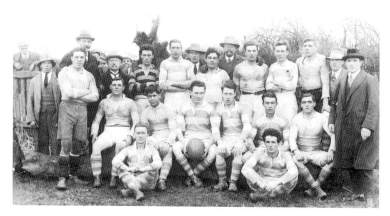

Another rugby photograph taken by local photographer Harold Stokes, 14 March 1925. Again, the team played against was Stroud 'A'. This time it was a home game and the Cheltenham team won. The team's full name was Cheltenham North Ward RFC more often abbreviated to Cheltenham North. The North Ward covered St Peter's and the area of Cheltenham known as Lower Dockem. Cheltenham North players were very much a working class group of men. The team played in blue shirts with white hoops and this photograph was taken on a field at Gardner's Lane, renowned for its uneven surface. Holding the ball is the captain, A. Barnett. Standing on the left, middle row, is Bill Burford, who was a legend of Cheltenham Rugby. The club's headquarters was The Railway Inn, Tewkesbury Road.

Above: During 1937 there were many parties held all over Cheltenham to celebrate the coronation of King George VI. This is Waterloo Street and a photograph of several families from St Peter's parish, with the vicar, Revd Richards. Some of the children have been identified: Joyce Cummings, Barbara Cummins, Rosie Green, Jim Green, Harry Green, Olive Green, Barbara Green, Peter Green, Doreen Green, Ken Jakeway, Phyllis Jenkins, Betty Powell, Desmond Powell, Ken Russell, Len Tomlin, Marjori Tomlin, Peter Wakefield and Pam Wilmore.

Right: Christmas good wishes sent from 'your loving son Bill' to 'Mother' (Mrs Skinner, 22 Hungerford Street), dated 31 October 1943. Bill was 1198783 L.A.C. Skinner W. serving with the RAF India Command. William Alfred Ernest Skinner was born 17 August 1910. Before the war he was employed for twelve years as gardener/chauffeur to Mr George Strick of Lanesfield, Lansdown Road. He joined the RAF in 1940 and was employed as a Nursing Orderly during the whole of his service, serving in India from February 1942 to March 1945. He survived the war and returned to the St Paul's area of Cheltenham.

It was party time again in 1945. This area of Cheltenham had suffered during the war and in Waterloo Street they were happy to celebrate VE Day. Some of the children photographed at the party in 1937 are now young adults. In this photograph, taken with St. Peter's in the background, the following have so far been identified: Granny Attwood, Marion Attwood, Harold Attwood, Iris & Sheila Cummings, Harry Cummins, Mrs Cummins, Barbara Cummins, Mrs Pearce, Mrs Taylor, Mrs Welch and Pam Wilmore.

In 1953 there was another Coronation to celebrate, this time for Queen Elizabeth II. The ladies of Waterloo Street put on their posh frocks and party hats and a whole new generation of children donned fancy dress. Here we see a group of mainly adults, in which the following have been identified: Granny Attwood, Doug Bowd, Albert Cummings, Iris Cummings, Joyce Cummings, Mr Jefferies, Mrs Jefferies, Mrs Matthews, Basil Matthews, Mrs Pearce, John Pearce, Betty Powell, Dorothy Richards, Evan and Mrs Williams, Mrs Williams carrying Barbara Cummings, Doreen Williams, Vic Williams, On the cover of this book the children can be seen smiling and laughing, everyone obviously enjoying the occasion.

St Paul's Girls' School, *c.* 1910. About forty-eight girls are pictured in this classroom. The little girl in the third row from the front, second from left, is Violet Allsopp. Violet was born in 1901. Note the solid double desks with their attached upright bench seats and of course the inkwells. Many of the girls are wearing white smocks typical of this period. St Paul's Girls' School was built in 1898 and had 280 on the register in 1910. The headmistress for many years was Miss Sarah Blease.

These boys from St Paul's Practising School went to Westward Ho in 1939 for what was to be the last school trip before the war. The photograph was provided by Trevor Hall in Australia. Les Cummings remembers the trips to Bideford, Appledore and Clovelly and the visits to a glove factory, a furniture factory and a lighthouse. They were shown a 'mothballed' merchant ship, *Elba*, which was soon to see action in the war. Boys on the trip included: David Basher, Les Cummings, Howard Feild, Peter Green, David Hall, Trevor Hall, Bill Harper, Reg Hayward, Bert Kent, Derek Maybury, John Morse, Peter Mustoe, Gerald Smith, Sid Sutherland, John Udolerous. Back right is Bill Grinnell, a student teacher, who went on to teach at Naunton Park School.

St Peter's Football Team 1920/21. William Alfred Cummings, the smartly dressed shorter gentleman, wearing a Silver War Badge in his lapel and standing next to the young lad in the striped shirt, was a referee and former St Peter's player. This badge, also known as the Wound Badge or Services Rendered Badge, was issued to men who had been honourably discharged and was highly valued by those who were given them. William's badge was issued on 9 September 1918. Like many young Cheltenham lads before the war, he had gone to South Wales to work in the mines. In 1914 William signed up for war duty at Abertillery. He had served four years and sixty-nine days in the Monmouthshire Regiment when he was discharged in 1918. The young lad next to William is Arthur Arkell, and next to him wearing the cap is Arthur's brother Tom.

This card was posted on 29 August 1913 to Mrs Northam in Penarth in South Wales. B. Stubbs writes from 50? Brunswick Street, 'Dear Auntie, We have just had these done I thought you might like one, it's very good of my husband & the car…'.

Cheltenham Church of England Normal College (for teacher training) was established in 1847 and in 1849 moved to the newly erected St Paul's College buildings on Swindon Road. In 1854, the Practising School, designed by G.F. Bodley, was opened at St Paul's College, in St Paul's Road. Initially, first-year college students did about a fortnight's teaching in the practising school and second-year students took charge of a division of the school for one week. However, increasingly it was felt that the school was small and that the experience to be gained from teaching there was limited. Students began to go elsewhere for training but the Practising School continued to provide education for local children until 1951. Following the closure of the Cheltenham Boys' Practising School and Swindon Road Boys' Secondary School, Elmfield Secondary Boys' School was formed.

St Paul's Welfare Party, 1965. If you were one of the children on this photograph the author would love to hear from you.

This group poses for a photograph in Burton Street outside The Welsh Harp before setting off on an outing in 1928. One little girl is carrying her bucket and spade so perhaps the outing is to the seaside. The baby sitting on his mother's lap is Les Cummings. His father, William Alfred Cummings, is standing behind. Note the fashionable array of hats worn by the ladies.

This outing from The Welsh Harp on 8 June 1932 was to Malvern, Coventry, Birmingham and Stratford-on-Avon. The photograph was taken by the St Paul's photographer Harold Stokes. The group appears to be all men apart from the two little girls. The man with a pocket watch and wearing a First World War badge in his lapel is William Cummings.

eight

Hester's Way, Arle and Swindon Village

Above: Staff of Cheltenham High Street Branch of Barclays Bank pictured in 1943. Mr Norman McK Hamilton, seconded to Cheltenham to manage the newly established sub-branch at Benhall for the American Forces, was the former Manager of the American Department of Barclays Bank, Chief Foreign Branch, Fenchurch Street, London. Included in the photograph are thought to be: Mr Josey, Miss Lancaster, Mr Simmons, Mr Tom Spearpoint and Mr Winterbourne. Mr Hamilton and his colleague Mr Lowe are sitting in the front row (Mr Hamilton on the left of the photograph). The Manager of Barclays Bank at 394 The Strand, High Street, Cheltenham through the war years was Mr Francis Joseph Addison.

Opposite above: This photograph was taken on 17 November 1943 at the temporary sub-branch of Barclays Bank Ltd, established at Benhall Farm for the benefit of the US Forces Services of Supply, based here from July 1942 to October 1944. Mr Norman McK Hamilton, father of Mrs Jean Goddard, who has supplied this photograph and the one above, was seconded to Cheltenham High Street Branch of Barclays Bank during the war from London, to manage this small sub-branch. The photograph shows Mr Hamilton and his colleague Mr Lowe, the cashier, also seconded from London, and three Forces personnel. Very little is known of this sub-branch of Barclays Bank and both Mrs Goddard and Barclays Bank archivists are anxious to have any information or photographs readers may be able to supply. The photograph tells us that the branch was opened on 30 August 1943 and opened for three hours daily during the week and for one hour on Saturdays. Jean's recollections of visiting Cheltenham as a young girl in 1943 are of the Railway Hotel where she stayed with her mother and 'candies'. Her father apparently enjoyed his secondment to Cheltenham, played bowls here and was a member of the Special Constabulary.

Opposite below: The time spent at Benhall Farm by the US Forces Services of Supply during the war is commemorated by a flagpole and plaque shown here.

Wood's Arle Farm Dairy, as advertised in *Cheltenham: The Garden Town*, published in 1907. Arle Farm had become the Home Farm in 1806, but in 1879 it was purchased by James Wood and became Arle Farm Dairy. James Wood died in 1905 and the farm passed to his descendants.

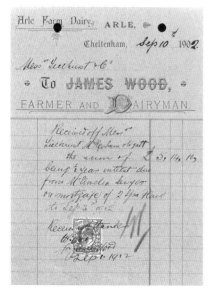

Invoice to James Wood, Farmer and Dairyman of Arle Farm Dairy, dated 10 September 1902.

In 1941, plans were being made with regard to housing needs and rebuilding plans for Cheltenham after the war. An estate was envisaged for the west side of the Borough, Hesters Way Estate. The difficulty was that the area to be utilised was good agricultural land and had been farmed for centuries. In the sixteenth century much of the land in Arle was owned or leased by the Gregory family and in 1591 John Gregory of Arle, husbandman, lived in Gregory's farmhouse – later Arle Farm. In the 1940s and '50s, land was acquired from the Arle House Estate, from Hesters Way Farm, Arle Court Farm and Arle Farm. Some of the land was taken by Compulsory Purchase, for sums of money generally considered to be unreasonable and unrealistic given the prosperity of the farms and the richness of the land, thus causing much controversy with the landowners.

Right: An early twentieth–century photograph of hay making at Arle Farm. 'James Wood, Arle Farm, Cheltenham' is clearly visible on the cart. Working on the farm at this time were Carter Wise and Carter Bullingham, and the horses included Violet, Bonny and Dumpty.

Below: Arle Farm, *c.* 1933. Farm workers with an old car made into a hay sweep.

The No. 8 bus photographed by the late Leslie Lapper on 23 May 1939. The driver is waiting with an empty bus at the terminus in Arle Road. Service 8 only ran between the Town Centre and Arle, via St George's Road and The Calcutta.

Left: Swindon, near Cheltenham, is the description on this early twentieth-century postcard. Nowadays, the area is always referred to as Swindon Village, to avoid any misunderstanding. This view, taken in Manor Road, coming from the junction in the village with Church Road and heading towards the Tewkesbury Road, looking down what is locally known as 'The Pitch', is not so familiar now. This photograph was taken when elm trees lined the road, many of which were later lost to Dutch Elm Disease.

Below: This genuine Victorian pram was still in use by a local family in the 1980s. The baby is Samantha Regan Woolfe.

This early postcard view of Swindon Church, *c.* 1900, was published in the Luna Series by
F.J. Waite, Cheltenham, and is unusual in that it was printed using a bright metallic colour
process. Frederick John Waite had studios in Cheltenham from the late 1880s. The cottage to the
left of the church is Church Cottage. The cottage and its garden belonged to the church and in
1909 the graveyard was extended to include part of the garden, although there was apparently no
dividing fence or wall between church and cottage until at least the late 1920s. The brother of a
man born in the cottage in the 1920s is said to have suffered a broken leg when a gravestone fell
on him.

The interior of the Church of St Lawrence, Swindon Village, photographed by E.M. Bailey,
c. 1910. The old oil lamps can be seen quite clearly hanging in the church. A local resident
remembers going with her mother to fill these lamps on Saturday mornings during the First
World War.

The little girl in the front of this group of schoolchildren is holding a slate with the words 'Swindon School'. The clothes would indicate that the date is probably around 1910 but no identification has been possible to date. If you can help, please contact the author.

Bus service 596 to Maud's Elm photographed at the Warden Hill terminus, c. 1970. This bus, registration number SHW 341, was new in 1954 and remained in service until 1972. For many years the buses went no further than Maud's Elm. Residents from Swindon Village had to walk to Maud's Elm to catch a bus to the town centre. Apparently, a number of people from the village used to cycle and leave their bicycles at the bungalow by the Folly playing field (Ivybrook). In June 1958, additional services were introduced and Swindon Village was one of the new areas to be covered. Service 6 ran from Warden Hill to Maud's Elm via the Town Centre and then on to Swindon Village. In 1967, the route numbers were changed and Cheltenham District services were allocated a range of numbers. Service 6 became Service 596.

The story surrounding a certain elm tree known as Maud's Elm, which stood in Swindon Road until it was struck by lightning and cut down in 1907, has been told many times (*Cheltenham Volume I* included a picture of the tree on page 60). This photograph is thought to have been taken just after the tree had been felled and shows men with axes sitting on the stump and a steam tractor behind them.

Little is known about this photograph of a group of men sitting on a pile of newly sawn wood. It was found with the above photograph and it is assumed that the men are sitting on planks of wood from the felled tree. Any information readers may be able to provide relating to the felling of Maud's Elm would be gratefully appreciated by the author.

Bibliography

The following publications have been the main sources of reference when compiling this volume:

Cheltenham Chronicle & Gloucestershire Graphic, 1904–30
Cheltenham & District Post Office Directory, 1891-2
Cheltenham Local History Society journals – various
Gloucestershire Echo & The Citizen newspapers – various
Griffith's New Historical Description of Cheltenham, 1826
Kelly's Directory of Gloucestershire & Cheltenham, from 1897
Slater's Commercial Directory, 1858-9
Swindon Village, Collections I-VI
The History of Hester's Way, Volumes 1-3
Who's Who in Cheltenham, 1911

Blake, Steven – *Cheltenham: A Pictorial History*
Blake, Steven – *Cheltenham's Churches and Chapels:* AD 773-1883
Brooks, Robin – *The Story of Cheltenham*
Clarke, A.K. – *A History of the Cheltenham Ladies' College: 1853-1979*
Devereux & Sacker – *Leaving all that was dear: Cheltenham and The Great War*
Fletcher, Susanne – *Charlton Kings*
Freeman, Peter – *How GCHQ came to Cheltenham*
Garrett, Doctor J.H. MD – *Cheltenham: The Garden Town* (various editions, 1901-1912)
Gill & Miller, – *Leckhampton*
Goding, John – *Norman's History of Cheltenham*
Hodsdon, James – *An Historical Gazetteer of Cheltenham*
Hughes, J.P. – *The Junior Rugby Clubs of Cheltenham, District and Combination*
Johnstone & Boothman – *The Cheltenham Ladies' College: A Brief History and Guide*
Mantle, Jonathan – *The Story of Cheltenham & Gloucester Building Society*
Martin, Colin – *Cheltenham's Trams & Early Buses*
Martin, Colin – *Cheltenham's Buses 1939-1980*
More, Charles – *The Training of Teachers 1847-1947*
Morgan, M.C. – *Cheltenham College: The First Hundred Years*
Osmond, Stephen E. – *A Chronology of Cheltenham 200* BC – AD *2000*
Paget, Mary – *A History of Charlton Kings*
Waller, Jill – *A Chronology of Trade and Industry in Cheltenham*